Stop Hating Your Job And Take Control Of Your Life

Shantnu Tiwari

Copyright © by Shantnu Tiwari 2016
ALL RIGHTS RESERVED
Without limiting the rights under copyright reserved above, no part of this book may be reproduced in any form or by any electronic or mechanical means, including information storage and retrieval systems, without permission in writing from the publisher, except by a reviewer, who may quote brief passages in a review.

DEDICATION

Dedicated to my wife Divya, without whose patient support this book would never have finished.

And let's not forget little Ojas!

Introduction (and not a boring one)

Yes, I know intros to books are usually boring, but do read this one. It'll tell you if this book is for YOU.

The book was inspired by two blog posts that took my website visitors from 2 per day to 25,000 in 24 hours, crashing my server. I got so many comments, I decided to address them in a book. The blog posts are there in the appendix and don't overlap with the main material, so are still useful.

This book was originally published as *Stop Being the Hamster*. This was meant to be a cute reference to the fact most people live their lives as hamsters, running on the wheel of work and its associated bullshit politics, till they die of exhaustion or a lack of peanuts, or both.

Yes, a very cute title.

Also, a failure.

Most people didn't understand the reference (without reading the book), and thought it was a book about cute hamsters doing cute tricks.

So I'm renamed the book, and added

this introduction. Before we go ahead, I'd like to explain my philosophy a bit. No, not Plato and stuff. I'm talking about what I believe.

I believe that if you hate your job and are stuck in a dead end one, it's partly your fault. Of course, the system is crooked too, and I show you how (or why) it became that way. But ultimately, you are a part of the system, so you share the blame if all you do is moan, moan, and moan.

My whole point in the book is, grow up and take control of your life. If you like this thinking, read on.

Welcome to the Zoo

Welcome to the Workplace Zoo, ladies and gentlemen. We will tour this wild place in our little safari car, inspired from the movie Jurassic Park. Keep your eyes open, and you might just see a few rare office animals.

If you look to the right, you will see hundreds of hamsters. All they do is run round and round for a few pellets of food. Yes, even we are surprised at how stupid these creatures are, but there you go. The more they run, the more profit we make and often we reward them with a pat on the head.

No, don't put your hand out of the car. We are now passing through the monkey cage. All the monkeys you see working in the cubicles started out as hamsters, but over time became angry and aggressive. They still work in cubicles but will attack anyone who comes near, including customers and other employees. They often damage our office systems, but still manage to do some work, so we keep them around.

Ah, we are now entering the

management section. Cover your heads, ladies and gentlemen. Those you see flying above you are the seagulls. They follow the seagull management style— they fly towards you, crap on you, and then fly away. Yes, please protect yourself from the pearls of wisdom they are about to drop on you.

Why are there so many who hate their jobs, but still put up with it?

Why do so many people hate their jobs? Why do they sit in their cubicles, staring at their watches, waiting for the day to end?

Whose fault is it? Your parents? Society? Evil aliens from the planet Moboo who have brainwashed us? (Yes.)

The default response in this situation is to blame the teachers and schools. But teachers are overworked and under appreciated as it is. Besides, their hands are tied. They are under constant pressure to cook the exam results. Rather than teaching us anything, a teacher's job has become to make us remember useless facts so that we get more and more marks on more and more useless exams, making the education department look good.

I think the problem is that most

people are content with life. They like (if not love) their jobs. In many careers, especially those with unions, career progression is automatic. Other professions—like doctors, teachers, firefighters—are filled with people who love what they do. Not every teacher wants to become the head teacher, not every doctor wants to become the surgeon general (and nor is it possible nor desired. I want a great doctor to heal me, a great teacher to teach my kids. I don't want greedy, career-driven selfish types around my children. Or as they are also called: bankers).

There are plenty of jobs, mainly in government, but in the private sector as well, where your job may be boring but is fairly stable and safe. You know that if you turn up every day, you will retire in thirty years with a fixed pension.

My book isn't for those people.

In fact, if you are one of those content people, first of all, congratulations. Second, please contact me for a refund.

My book is for those of us stuck in corporate jobs, who have no job stability, but whose job still sucks. Those who have lost job stability and lifelong careers and gotten nothing but cheesy MBA talk in return.

The problem is our children are being trained for the late 19th workplace, when the factory model was in power.

In the factory model of production, you turned up, did the same thing over and over for ten hours, took your lunch break, filled out your time sheets, and went home. It was the same for companies. They would build a widget for a dollar, sell it for a dollar fifty. Fifty pence profit per widget, sell a thousand a day, that's a five-hundred dollar a day profit. Minus three hundred for wages and expenses, and you are looking at a good margin. Everyone knew what their role was. The workers made widgets, the salesmen sold them, the managers sat in closed rooms and had meetings.

And now, the whole world has changed. Except for the managers. They still sit in closed rooms and have meetings all day, which gives them tremendous job security.

But even though the world changed, the way of thinking, the ingrained habits and patterns society has, haven't. These patterns are subconscious, which is why it's useless blaming teachers or parents or politicians for them. (But feel free to blame the evil aliens from Moboo).

So even though we no longer live in a society where turning up and making widgets all day is the normal pattern of working, this is how we are trained. Everything, from our schools, our universities, our job system, our banks, everything, is designed to function like a widget factory.

At school, you sit passively while someone goes blah blah blah. And how are our universities different? I laugh when people make the claim that universities make you cultured and sophisticated. How does sitting in a class and hear some teaching assistant (because professors no longer teach) blabber on for fifty minutes make you sophisticated? Hitting yourself in the face with a dead fish would make you more sophisticated; plus, you could eat the fish for lunch.

And it's the same with our jobs. Turn up to work, do what you're told, go home.

Like hamsters. You run round and round in your little wheel, going nowhere with your career.

This is where the concept of the

nine-to-fiver comes in. I personally hate that term, as some of the most productive and intelligent people I've met are nine to fivers. They do their job really well so they can leave on time and spend time with their family. And on the other spectrum, a lot of lazy people will spend the mornings chatting and messaging on the computer and then stay late to impress the boss.

Which is why I hate the term *nine to five*. So I am coining the term *cubicle hamster* (or *corporate hamster*). A related animal is the cubicle monkey, who is like the hamster except that while the hamster still has hope, the monkey has become hopeless and, as a result, turned aggressive (or even worse, passive-aggressive).

A cubicle hamster is someone who sits in his/her cubicle, does what s/he is told, and is rewarded with peanuts at the end of the day. A cubicle hamster could be a call centre worker, a highly paid engineer, an accountant, or a graphic designer. They are usually good at one technical thing, whether it is programming, designing websites, or running on a wheel.

Why do I call them hamsters? Because they have no control over their life. When the circus master cracks his whip, they must get up and dance. Actually, I am being insulting. Hamsters can't be fired randomly or forced to sit through a humiliating performance review, designed only to show you why you don't deserve a bonus this year.

After a lifetime of being crushed, the hamsters turn into monkeys. They start attacking people, damaging stuff. Cubicle monkeys are a million times worse than hamsters.

If there are any monkeys in the crowd, I apologise for comparing you to employees. You do not deserve it, I know. But for some reason, many office workers think they are better than monkeys.

You have met many cubicle monkeys in your life. You probably are one yourself. Every time you phone a call centre and someone hangs up on you mid-sentence, you know you just talked to a cubicle monkey who has been told to cut conversations after two minutes, even if the problem hasn't been solved. The corporate monkey is the bank clerk who, while cleaning their nose with their finger, tells you he will have to reject your application because you didn't fill out page 50 of 200 correctly. It is the estate agent/lawyer who will bully you into filling your forms on time, and then sit on them for weeks.

And in each case, the person is doing exactly what they have been told. They may hate their job, they may realise they are doing the wrong thing, but they are helpless to do anything.

But this book isn't about complaining about the corporate world. There are a lot of other books about that. This book isn't about teaching you some cool trick that will make you rich in only twenty-one days. I don't have any such secret, and even if I had, I wouldn't share it with you.

Instead, I want you to learn and accept that the system is screwed up because the people inside it make it so. And that includes you. Yes, you. You are as much a part of the problem as any evil boss you may hate. You take a bunch of people trained to think in the industrial age, where making widgets was the only thing to do, and you put them in front of a computer, where they have to make actual decisions based on data that changes constantly. What do you expect? Rainbows and butterflies?

You are a part of the problem, too.

What have you done recently to improve your company or yourself? Moaning or complaining doesn't count. If you haven't done anything, why should someone else?

But my job isn't to blame you, either. I want you to see that you are a part of the problem. You have grown in an environment which taught you how to behave in a world that existed two hundred years ago. So if you want to escape the cubicle, the first thing you need to do is change your thinking patterns. You might not be able to change your current workplace, but you can certainly change yourself and move to something better.

Darwin's Survival of the Fittest gets thrown about a lot (even though technically it wasn't Darwin who said it). Especially by the banker types, who use it as an excuse to justify their bloated salaries (because in their world, moving money from one pocket to another is such hard work that it justifies a two-million-dollar bonus).

But if you look at what survival of the fittest meant originally, it means that the environment in which beings exists keeps changing all the time. At any given time, the creature that bests fits the current environment will thrive. So when there was plenty of oxygen and food, huge dinosaurs thrived. When food became scarce, smaller mammals, including the ones that eventually became humans, survived.

In the same way, the environment in our modern society has changed. But we are still acting like we are living in the mid-nineteenth century. We are out of touch with our environment, which is why so many people are miserable at their jobs. Rather than blaming the environment, try to change yourself to adapt. And that is the goal of this book. To take you from a corporate monkey, who can't do anything without the circus master's approval, to someone in charge of their own destiny.

They got you early

It was Hammy the hamster's first day at work. He was really excited. He had just spent two hundred thousand dollars in getting his Masters in Running on Hamster Wheel. It would take him fifty-seven years to pay back the debt, but he was okay with it. After all, his parents, his teachers, the career counsellor, the guys on TV, they had all said the same thing: Go to university, and you are made for life. He had put in the hours. All he had to do now was wait for the money to roll in.

Many people hate their jobs and wonder where it all went wrong. But the problem is it was never right to begin with. It's like trying to build a castle of sand on top of a sleeping man. No matter how careful you are, the whole thing will crumble down at one point.

You were set up for failure ever since you were in grade school. Really, you ask. Really, I say. What did they tell you from the day you were tall enough to get your butt off the ground and start walking? "Go to school, go to a good university, and you have it made."

And hence thousands of hopeful, naïve kids turn up at their first day at work, all wide eyed and innocent. They have been swallowing the line since kindergarten. They did all the right things, went to the right universities, dutifully sat in lecture halls and listened to the teaching assistant drone on and on. Now the universe owes them a career. Not just a job, but a real career. Millionaire by thirty, top of the industry by forty. And if you are a man, you have the added bonus of deserving a hot trophy girlfriend. And why not? You did all they asked for, didn't you?

The elder generation, especially the ones in power, take great fun in calling the younger generation lazy good for nothings. The word *hipster* is thrown about a lot. Look at these self-entitled hipsters, thinking the world owes them a living. Cue lots of smirking.

But who is the real hipster? The twenty-year-old kid who just got into a fifty-thousand-dollar debt studying English literature, or his professor, who earns upwards of a hundred thousand, and who convinced the youngster that getting thousands into debt was the best thing he could do for his career? And the same professor who then smirks and laughs at "all these damn kids with their sense of entitlement"?

For the real question is: how is an English professor qualified to give anyone career advice? (And I'm not picking on English teachers. Replace them with philosophy or art professors, if you are so inclined). If you have an eighteen-year-old kid, lost about what to do with his life, is the best advice you can give him, "Sit in a big lecture hall and try to stay awake while someone who couldn't accomplish anything in his own life will try to teach you how to live your life? And oh yes, you will have to spend fifty-sixty thousand dollars for this honour?"

Or would you tell him, "Learn to sell, kid. Learn to market. Talk to people, see how they struggle, and learn how you can help them get rid of their problems. Learn that people will pay good money to solve their pains."

The game is rigged. By the time you graduate from university, you are tens of thousands of dollars in debt. You have no option but to work for the man, accepting whatever bread crumbs are thrown your way.

By the time you realise you have been played, you are in your late thirties, with a huge mortgage and three kids. And you see these fresh-faced pimply kids coming up, like a lambs to slaughter. So you take out your sharpest knife and give your best smile.

"Listen, kids. You really need to go to university if you want to succeed in life."

But let's stop that line of thought. Like I mentioned at the beginning, I am not here to blame. Most people in society will go on accepting the subconscious programming they have been spoon-fed since they learnt how to use the toilet without mommy's help. What I can do is show you how you can fight the programming and make your own rules. And I don't say that in a sulky teenage way. "You're not the boss of me! I'll do what I want."

Not really, as most of these rebels are as much a part of the system they are rebelling against. They all wear the same branded clothes, helping the same corporate bourgeois they supposedly hate.

When I say make your own rules, I

mean the subconscious mental rules that govern our thinking. Things like "I better push my head down and take it like a man. After all, the alternative could be worse."

Hammy was running on the wheel. It had all he had been doing in the last few days. But it seemed to be making no difference. He looked at the hamsters around him. They seemed to be doing the bare minimum and only put on speed when the boss hamster came around. Hammy wondered if there was a point to all this. Meanwhile, his parents were pressuring him to get married and buy a house. Everyone else his age had done it. He needed to stop acting the child.

There is hope for Hammy yet. Do you see the subconscious programming? Hammy must marry and buy a house, not because he feels it's the correct time, but because "that's the way it's always been done." Go against society's programming and they will fight you tooth and nail.

But Hammy isn't helpless, even though it may seem that way now. Your whole life, you were trained to be a corporate monkey. You now need to get off the hamster wheel and learn to control your own destiny.

Lies they told you

Ever since you were a kid, you have been lied to. The biggest lie was that going to university would make your career, but that wasn't the only one. Here are a few more you have been force-fed:

The world owes you a good living

You are probably reading this thinking, who would be stupid enough to believe that? Not you! You know that you have to work hard to succeed.

Answer this honestly: Have you ever daydreamed about becoming a millionaire by thirty? Read all these business articles that give you the secret of success and wondered how you'll apply it?

Well then, congratulations. You fell into the trap.

Many intellectual types laugh at the fashion magazines that sell the idealised image of how women should look (after they have been photoshopped). Yet isn't that how most business books and magazines work? By giving you an idealised version of setting up a business? "Why, I set up a landing page and within an hour got eleventy million sign ups, and just six months later, am planning to retire, dump my wife for a super model, and travel the world in my gold-plated yacht."

If you have ever read a business book and become inspired, you have fallen into this trap. Why? Because you just stopped at being inspired. You didn't do anything after that, did you? I know this because you are reading my book instead of managing your business. See, I'm smart, ain't I?

If you work hard, you have it made.

This lie is repeated not just by the corporate types, but by venture capitalists as well. If you think of it, it's quite strange. You would think the corporate types and venture capitalists would be enemies, so why are they reading from the same textbook?

There was a blogger recently who said something like, "You damn kids, stop complaining. If you want to succeed, you need to get your head down and be prepared to work eighteen-hour days. That's the way it's always been done. The only people who make it are the ones who sleep under their desks."

But the blogger made the mistake of quoting Jamie Zawinsky, who immediately responded. Even the title of his post was amusing. "Watch a VC use my name to sell a con":

"He's trying to make the point that the only path to success in the software industry is to work insane hours, sleep under your desk, and give up your one and only youth, and if you don't do that, you're a pussy. He's using my words to try and back up that thesis.

I hate this, because it's not true, and it's disingenuous.

What is true is that for a VC's business model to work, it's necessary for you to give up your life in order for him to become richer.

Follow the fucking money. When a VC tells you what's good for you, check your wallet, then count your fingers.

He's telling you the story of, "If you bust your ass and don't sleep, you'll get rich" because the only way that people in his line of work get richer is if young, poorly-socialized, naive geniuses believe that story! Without those coat-tails to ride, VCs might have to work for a living. Once that kid burns out, they'll just slot a new one in.

I did make a bunch of money by winning the Netscape Startup Lottery, it's true. So did most of the early engineers. But the people who made 100x as much as the engineers did? I can tell you for a fact that none of them slept under their desk."

http://www.jwz.org/blog/2011/11/watch-a-vc-use-my-name-to-sell-a-con/

Why did I bring this up?

To show you that just starting your own business may not be enough to escape being a hamster. You'll go from being the corporate hamster to the venture capitalist's hamster. (If I was a rude person, I'd say bum boy, but I'm not, so I won't).

The system is fair

"Golly gee, Batman! We live in a fair and wonderful world. All we have to do is work hard and all will be rewarded. The wonderful wizard of Oz will give us our heart's desire."

I know none of you believe that. Because you bought this book, right? No, you are more likely to believe…

The system is unfair, so no use taking part

"Boo hoo hoo! The system is crooked, man! Only the suits get the top jobs. Us geeks are like, screwed man. Why even bother, dude? Let's go back to watching to our TV."

This feeling is brought out by a sense of powerlessness. If nothing you do matters, what is the use of doing anything? Cynicism is in fashion. Being sarcastic and insulting is considered cool. But while this might make you cool with thirty-something professor types, it will not help your goal of escaping the cubicle. The system is crooked, but you still have to take part. As I will say later on, if you try to hide in your cubicle, all you will accomplish is letting the loud mouths control your career.

Lies Hollywood told you

This section gets its own chapter, as even though Hollywood has nothing to gain by feeding us bullshit, lazy storytelling and a short attention span means they have spoonfed you more than one lie which you have accepted as the gospel truth. Since you have been watching TV since childhood, many of these lies have become a part of your subconscious, and so need special surgery to remove.

Hollywood has given us a very terrible image of how the corporate world works. For one, the hero/heroine always has this one big presentation they have to give to a client/their boss, and everything hinges on this one presentation. Ask yourself: How many times has your entire career depended on one big meeting? I was once a part of a meeting with a client that was worth several million dollars. And it got cancelled at the last moment because we found out (shock! horror!) that the software we were trying to sell them didn't actually work. It wasn't a big deal, and the client was happy to reschedule. That was an extreme case, but normally, our work consists of a lot of small, never-ending tasks, not one big make-it-or-break-it meeting. So why does every Hollywood movie use this concept?

It's because that's how Hollywood works. Writers and directors have meetings with producers/studios, and the whole funding for the movie, which could be in the hundreds of millions, depends on that one meeting, which may be over in ten minutes. So they think that the rest of us work that way as well. Think about that: Hollywood writers have no idea how you work and live. In their world, computers explode when they crash, you have to cock your gun every time you want to shoot it, and alien motherships run Windows Vista (because you can upload viruses to them). These are the people you are taking career advice from?

What happens in the Hollywood version of work?

1. The boss is an obvious bully, who screams at people, pinches bums, gets drunk, and acts outrageously.

Ask yourself this: How many times have you met anyone like this in any workplace in any country since the 1950s? Again, Hollywood people are rude, loud, and act like jerks, so they assume that's how your boss behaves as well.

2. The hero is the hero (Yes, I know. I'm not good with words, which makes me uniquely qualified to write this book). What I mean is the whole world revolves around him. The script is grabbed by the neck and forced to dance to the hero's tune. What's wrong with that, you ask? The problem is that people expect that's how real life will work as well.

What happens in movies? The hero is misunderstood. He tries to work hard, but everyone mocks him. The hot girl ignores him.

The hero continues doing what he's being doing. He continues being the good guy and slowly, people start noticing him. Clients want to do business with him, the CEO becomes his best chum, even the hot girl starts noticing him.

What's wrong with this picture?

For one, just continuing doing what you are doing will not get you promoted. Is that what you see around you? When you go to a checkout queue at a superstore and see the cashier scanning your shopping, do you go, "Hmm, she sure is a fast scanner. At this rate, she can serve ten customers a minute. She should be promoted to shop manager!" Or do you just ignore her, because you expect her to work that fast? And why would it be different for you and your boss?

3. The Karate Kid effect

What's the Karate Kid effect?

Those of you who just dropped from the planet Mars, first of all, welcome to Earth. Second, Karate Kid was a movie from the 1980s that I didn't particularly like but is considered a cult classic by many people. It features the classic good guy, i.e., a loser kid with no redeeming qualities. In real life, he would be flipping burgers, but since this is a movie, they have to give him a reason to change. So they create these over-the-top bullies who use karate to beat our hero up. The bullies were over the top because if you acted like that in real life, you'd go to prison and get sued. Especially the karate teacher, who would know that the police take a dim view of encouraging kids to beat each other up, not to mention no one would sell him insurance.

But that's not the problem of the Karate Kid. The problem is, in the movie, the kid meets a magical Asian man who teaches him a super-secret martial art system. And rather than spending years learning the basics of karate, and then some more years mastering the art, he spends all his time doing wax on, wax off (Google it if you haven't seen the movie). And just by doing some light exercise, he manages to master the art and beat up people who have been practising it for years.

This seems to be the lesson of many movies. In Avatar, Jake just lands on the planet and manages to think of stuff the locals hadn't been able to think, and fight in ways they never dreamed of. In the 2009 reboot of Star Trek, Kirk, a kid who barely passed his exams, suddenly gets command of a whole ship and defeats an enemy no one else has been able to. Before any Star Trek fans send me angry letters, look at how the modern navy works. Can you imagine some hot-blooded kid becoming the captain of a nuclear submarine or an aircraft carrier? If you look at the people who command these ships, they are often older men who have spent years studying the whole ship. Many are engineers, if not by degree, then by the special training they get. Would someone like Kirk be put in command of a nuclear submarine, no matter how bad the situation was?

But that's not how our Hollywood heroes work. No, sir. They just do wax on, wax off. They don't spend years studying the fine details of their craft. They don't pass certification exams. They never struggle with politics. They don't spend years doing the same thing over and over and over till someone notices them. No siree. You see, they are the chosen ones. And the chosen ones get everything by default. Look at the biggest example of the Chosen One: Harry Potter. Not only is he the best wizard (even though he has no experience of magic, as he didn't grow up in a magical family, and, unlike Herminone, doesn't spend any time doing research), he is great at the game of Quidditch, even though he has never played it, while other wizard kids have been playing it for years. Again, to compare to the normal world, can you imagine an eleven year old picking up a golf set and starting to hit holes in one on the first try? And before you shove Tiger Woods in my face, Tiger spent his whole childhood, whole days, evenings, and weekends practising non-stop. He didn't become a world champion because he was the chosen one.

What's the problem with this thinking? The problem is real life is not a Hollywood story. You are not the hero of your own epic saga. You are not the chosen one. Since you are reading this book, chances are you aren't very bright, because you chose to take advice from someone like me, instead of, you know, smart people who actually know stuff.

Successful people in the real world don't wait for magical foreigners or bored angels to teach them anything. They just put their posterior on the chair and get working.

Whose fault is it?

Quick question: What determines your worth in society?

A. Your job

B. What university you went to

C. What car you drive and how hot your partner is

D. Let's be honest. Who you know, not what you know.

Hammy wasn't happy. He had been running the same wheel for three years, but he was still the Junior Hamster. He couldn't understand it. He had done everything they asked. He stayed late, finished his assignments on time, ran round and round and round on that treadmill. So why wasn't he getting that promotion? Or a pay raise that wasn't half of inflation?

Before we go further, we'll take a little detour into a bit of anthropology. At least, the kindergarten version of it.

Thousands of years ago, when dinosaurs ruled the earth and humans hunted wild carnivorous sheep on the back of dinosaurs (I got my history lesson from the Flintstones, as you may have guessed), humans lived in tribes. Life was tough. There was no dental floss, and if you wanted a midnight snack, you had to get up and kill your own lion to make one.

Now imagine this tribal society. Every day, they hunt or gather what they can. If they don't find anything, they starve. Life is short and tough.

In this mix arrives a hipster. He wears his rag at an angle. He insists they only eat vegetarian animals like sheep, and only pick organic nuts. He tells everyone that he deserves all the women of the tribe because of how nice a person he is. Inside, he is very beautiful. He is a unique snowflake. He refuses to hunt, stating that he is an intellectual, a man of science, and not a brute. Or perhaps he claims to be an artist.

What do you think will happen?

A. He will be chosen as the leader of the tribe. The tribe will recognise how smart he is, how beautiful he is on the inside. Because that's all that matters, right? What you are on the outside is just a reflection of what you are on the inside.

B. The tribe clubs him on the head and leaves him as a meal for the lions.

Now fast forward to today.

You have a pretty young boy/girl, fresh out of university. Their whole life, they have been told they are special, God's gift to humankind. They have it made. They are beautiful on the inside, if not on the outside.

And this person goes to the real world and reality slaps them in the face. They realise that no one cares about them. At all. And then they become depressed, or passive-aggressive, or both. And then the tribe throws them to the lions.

What, did you think that just because we have moved out of the forests, become civilised, just because we eat with a fork and knife and drink our lattes with straws and say, "Excuse me, ole chap" when we fart (or is that just me?), that we have escaped the tribe? Look around. People are fighting in the name of their religion, sect, country, even their stupid football club. What is that if not tribal mentality?

Even though we live in cities with millions of people, we act as a tribe.

Now, the next time you are depressed because you aren't getting that promotion, or are not getting your dream job, ask yourself this: What do you bring to the table? What's your contribution to the tribe?

Imagine you are stuck in a cave, with lions hunting you and the tribe inside. Is your fancy university degree, your cool car, or that heart-touching poetry you wrote going to save you? What do you bring to the table?

The tribe protects its own, but it is also very harsh towards those it thinks are dragging it down. Through millions of years of evolution, we have learnt how to protect the tribe, even if it means sacrificing a few members. In the Middle Ages, when plague and other diseases were widespread, people found a simple way to fight diseases. They would dump the sufferers out of the town and leave them to die. And while it may seem cruel to you today, the method worked. It had a lot of false positives. People with simple skin rashes found themselves starving to death because the villagers thought they had the plague.

The tribe tries to protect itself while trying to grow and expand at the same time. If you are helping the tribe, you will get rewarded. Otherwise, you will be dumped for the lions. It's that simple.

One of the reason for all the hate towards the so-called hipsters (so-called because no one can agree on the definition of a hipster) is due to the belief, correct or not, that hipsters live their lives at the expense of others. Society is still very cruel towards those it doesn't feel is contributing.

Sure, a few people might manipulate the system and get rich through screwing society. Slum lords and bankers come to mind, especially as both of them get rich by leeching off the real productive people. But such leeches are usually squished, sometimes with extreme violence, as in the case of the French Revolution. Ultimately, society only rewards those it feels are contributing most to it. Keep that in mind. That's why you have websites like Uniform Dating, an actual dating website that helps women find men in uniform, from police officers to firemen. Why isn't there a Nerd Dating, or World of Warcraft Top Scorer dating website? Or I-know-how-to-program-computers-and-so-I-must-be-attractive dating website? That's because the tribe values those who protect it (police and firefighters) above those who make crappy websites that crash ten times a day. Which is the why the lowly paid firefighter has a higher social standing than the better-paid programmer, or the well-paid doctor has a much higher social standing than the obscenely paid banker. That's why a stay-at-home mother gets more respect than some unemployed hipster who spends all his time protesting against real or perceived evils. Even though both of them aren't working, one is contributing to society. Taking care of kids may look like a minor contribution to society (since there are millions of them running about, keeping McDonald's in business), but it is a contribution society values above all else.

    Because the tribe knows who is protecting it. When the lions are attacking and the tribe can only protect a few, it will protect the children and the few people it believes are helping the most. Everyone else will be left to die, even intentionally killed so that the lions get their food and leave the tribe alone.

    Most people in modern society are extremely polite, so they will never say this to your face. But if you become the guy who isn't helping the tribe, the tribe will dump you in society's garbage can. You must have seen it. It is full of people who had so much hope and potential, the ones everyone said would make it, the ones expected to be millionaires by thirty, but the ones who now spend their time drunk in bars, if not worse?

Now you are wondering, how does this apply to me? If you are reading this book, chances are you are not an attractive firefighter or nurse. You probably work in an office, where you spend most of the day moving files from pile A to pile B to the shredder. You contribute nothing to society, only to the corporation and its executives (who, in the true spirit of the religion of shareholder primacy, use that money to line their own pockets). You most likely never see your customers, and the only contribution your work makes to society is when you remember to throw the can of juice in the recycling bin.

And that's one of the reasons you are so miserable in your job. You make no visible contribution to the tribe, and to the tribe, you are invisible. And since you are invisible, you don't exist.

So whose fault is it?

You hate your job. You can't tolerate another second staring at the clock, pretending to work but secretly hating your life.

Whose fault is it?

You know the usual answers: greedy managers, selfish bosses, no one understands you, yadda yadda.

What if I were to say it's your fault?

You are a part of the system, right? You are not a helpless victim. You are not a poor dear, a tender flower that sways with the wind. If you are reading this book, chances are you are not a poor Third World farmer at the mercy of the weather. You are most likely a white collar worker, and compared to the rest of the world, your living standard is amongst the top in the world. You don't have to worry about finding clean water, saving your children from malaria, trying to survive the various factions fighting a civil war in your country, risk being stoned to death because you offended the majority religion. So why are you miserable?

Like I have been saying, my job isn't to blame you. Rather, it's to give you the tools to discover why you hate your job so much, and then fix it.

There are many reasons why such a large percentage of people hate their jobs.

Some of which are your fault, some of which aren't. But before you can fix your problems, you need to be a hundred percent sure, in your own mind and heart, that you aren't a cause of the problem. Which is why I say there are many factors. Maybe your boss is a jerk. But maybe you are a spoilt brat who expects to be treated like daddy/mommy's little darling, and can't seem to understand that in the real world, no one cares about you. See Rule Number One: No one cares about you. I have no way of knowing which is the truth. I hope I will give you the tools so you can make the decision for yourself. How will you know if you made the correct one? You will stop hating your job and feeling miserable all the time. That's the golden test. But for that to work, you need to be really honest with yourself. Because if you are the problem, you need to fix that. If the job is the problem, you need to change it. But if the problem lies within you and you change the job, you will face the same problems again at the new job. **Changing the environment does not fix your problems.**

It may not be completely your fault. A poll says that only 30 percent of the people are engaged in their jobs. That's 70 percent of people who turn up at work, hate it, and do a shoddy job, doing just the bare minimum to not get fired. Remember that the next time you phone a call center. Your problem maybe urgent and causing you to lose time and money. For the call center worker, it's likely just a nine-to-five job. They don't care. They are probably penalized if they care too much, as if they actually help you, their time per incident goes up.

And why does some corporation care about some stupid metric like time per incident? Do they think that I have nothing better to do except calling them and wasting their time, increasing their time per whatever?

They care because of the weird history of the corporation. Let's start with their fault, i.e., the reason why so many jobs are terrible. Many of today's problems started in the 1970s, when the idiotic shareholder value maximisation theory came into fashion.

Where they went wrong

The corporation: A history

Corporations are legal entities. That is, they are independent of the people who run them. They can enter into contracts, and can buy/sell property/goods. If the corporation makes a mistake, you can't sue the managers (unless they are doing something clearly illegal). You can only sue the corporation itself.

In the UK, there are several consumer protection programs on BBC. Watchdog and Rogue Traders to mention a few. They go after businesses that have been screwing their customers. One thing these firms do if they get sued is just close down and open with another name. Which is not a good idea, as BBC just tracks down the directors and shames them on TV. But it just goes to show: As long as the directors aren't doing anything overtly criminal, they are not responsible for their companies' actions, even though they were directing and controlling that company. This point is important to understand.

The limited liability of corporations

is actually a very good idea, if used honestly. It means that you can start risky ventures and only lose the money you invested. As opposed to gambling on the share market, where you can lose a million dollars for every dollar you invested. Just ask the bankers who caused the 2007 crash.

Corporations worked well, which is why they became so successful. But in the 1970s, due to oil shortages, the economy was really depressed (for those who don't know, the belief in the '70s was that we would run out of oil soon, bringing about an end to civilization. Mad Max, made in the '80s, was based on this theme). The stock market wasn't rising as fast as some people wanted.

At this time, a new theory called the shareholder value maximisation was formulated. The theory was very average and published in a below-average journal. But it came at the right time and found favour with a few elite. And soon, shareholder primacy became the new religion of the market. Managers, who for so long had been working so hard for average pay, around thirty to forty times the pay of the lowest employee, suddenly realized that they needed to be paid a hundred or a thousand times more to do the same job. The thinking was that if managers were asked to share in the profit, they would be more interested in making money for the shareholders.

So how do you think it worked out?

You already know how it did if you have ever even looked at a newspaper from twenty meters away.

While the average Return on Investment from investing in stock has gone down from 6 percent to 1.3 percent from 1965 to 2009, the CEO-to-worker ratio has gone up more than 1800% in the same time period.

In case you didn't understand the significance, managers are earning more and more salary for progressively lower profits. Both the long-term investors and the employees, as well as any other stakeholders, are getting screwed.

So who is making the money?

Shareholder maximisation was supposed to help the shareholders. Instead, it helps short term gamblers. Most investors only hold a stock for, on average, seven months. Companies are being run for the benefits of gamblers. Real investors are losing money, as the long-term pattern is towards the share price going down. At the same time, upper level managers are getting richer. Not just rich, but obscenely rich. There was a time when, if you wanted to be real rich, you started a business. Something big like trains, or knocking off Third World countries and installing puppet governments. Now, you become the CEO of some crappy little firm that doesn't make much profit but is very good at bribing politicians.

The fact is, the system is crooked. If CEOs don't cater to the gamblers, they can be and are kicked out. The company is run for the benefit of gamblers, who on average only hold interest for seven months. That means that every quarter, companies have to show a profit. The CEO's job is no longer to run a proper business but to run a gambling mill for addicts. It's worse. The CEO is a card shark who has teamed up with wolves to rob his own casino and its employees.

And let's not talk about the entitlement culture. Managers expect to be paid obscene amounts of money for doing less and less work.

But.

Before you go all angry and socialist

on me, remember that this is not about blame. You are not a social worker. It ain't your job to fix society. Sure, do good work, help when you can, but you can't change the system. If you feel really pissed, get your Mac out, buy an overpriced coffee, and go protest outside a bank.

So why did I tell you all that boring history? Cause you need to understand why the system is the way it is.

Managers are under pressure to produce short-term gains to satisfy their gambler investors. Proper research and development, customer care, and other good stuff takes time. So they take short cuts— cutting pay, treating customers like dirt, everything you ever read on Dilbert. They know they are doing wrong, but like drug dealers, they can't change. Which is actually a good thing, as it means the small guys can compete with them.

Where you go wrong

The previous chapter talked about where they went wrong. Now, I'd like to talk about where you can go wrong. While there are many reasons for failure, a few things really hold you back. Things like:

Being invisible

This disease has killed more victims than any other corporate disease till now. Also called the worker-sitting-in-the-cubicle-alone syndrome.

It's not enough to just do a good job. Your accomplishments need to be visible, too. If no one knows what a great job you've done, you will get zero credit.

Each one of us is shy to some degree, even the so-called extroverts. Most people have a sort of social phobia, the fear of being judged by strangers as well as people they know. If you have ever done something silly in public and spent the next two hours worrying about what people will think of you, so do you. Like I said, everyone has this fear of being judged to some degree, even your big-name celebrities. Look at these reality shows, where big-name celebrities come to dance or sing or act or whatever. When the time comes to score them, look at the faces of the celebrities. They are full of fear, the way you looked when you asked someone for your first date.

I was watching one of these celebrity dance shows, and the time came to score the dancer. Now, this dancer was a famous actress, more famous than the judges scoring her. Yet her face looked like she was going to cry. Like you had taken a toy away from a five year old for being naughty. And I was like, girl, why do you care what these judges think? You earn more than all of them combined. You are a superstar. And yet here she was, scared of losing a silly little dance contest that wouldn't affect her career in any way.

The problem with shyness or social phobia comes when it stops us from doing our normal work. I'll give my own example. I was (and still am) terribly shy. I am not the life of the party. When I enter a room, people don't go, "Hey! It's the Shantnu Man." I do not brighten up the room, and when I leave, 90 percent of the people don't even notice (I know this because I did a scientific survey after I had left the room).

But there was a time when it was worse. I would hide in my cubicle and keep my head down. I hoped no one would notice me and give me extra work. I was terrified of making a fool of myself.

Well, I succeeded in a way. I never made a fool of myself. But I didn't accomplish anything either, as I never got any cool assignments. I had become the cubicle monkey, the guy who danced when the circus master cracked the whip and was happy to eat peanuts all the time.

Many people are shy and want to avoid confrontation. The feeling is that *Those who stick their heads up get shot down.* And you know what? It is perfectly true. If you stand up and speak for yourself, there is a slight chance you will have to face embarrassment. I was like this for a long time. I kept my head low and only minded my own business. I was scared that if I said too much, I would be given extra work. Forced overtime. I had crazy fears of being pressed into a slave gang and being forced to work crazy hours.

Those fears were stupid. Other people got promoted, and they rarely worked long hours; not more than me, at least.

In this syndrome, you quietly work in your little cubicle, thinking you are safe from your evil bosses. What happens is the loud mouths and the won't-shut-ups start controlling your career.

You need to step out of your comfort zone now and then, make yourself feel uncomfortable. You need to let your opinion be heard. Don't speak just for the sake of speaking, but if you disagree with something, do speak out. If you think something could be improved, do say it, even if there is no chance of it happening. I remember giving a presentation on distributed version control systems in my company. Everyone shook their heads and said it was a good idea, but the body language of the senior managers was "Ain't gonna happen." But I gave the presentation anyway, as it did help the engineers.

If you want a quick tip to avoid becoming the cubicle monkey, it is this: At least once a week, voice your opinion (loudly, and not in an email or in your head) to your colleagues or boss. What will you say? Anything. You spent forty hours or more working at your place. Did you not find one thing you aren't happy with? Bring it up. Slowly get into a habit of doing this: Voicing your opinion, without being scared that you will be scolded.

It is also true that if you raise your head, some self-important twit will slap you down. However, if you never raise your head, you will be stuck at the level of the hamster: Always doing the same job over and over again, no promotion, bare minimum pay raises. You must have heard the saying: There is a price for following your dreams? Well, there is a price for not following your dreams too.

Not being assertive enough

Hammy was invited to a meeting with three senior managers. They were worried about why the project was late. The meeting started and Hammy sat quietly, bored out of his mind. One of the managers turned to him.

"And why is the project late, Mr Hamster?"

Hammy looked around, confused. He had been daydreaming till now. "Eh, what?"

"Why is the project late?"

Hammy's manager stepped in. "It was late because we misunderstood the specs."

Actually, the main reason was that the hardware had arrived late. But the manager forgot about that.

The senior manager nodded. Hammy breathed a sigh of relief. He had survived.

But actually, he hadn't. Two weeks later, Hammy's name was dropped from a promotion list. The managers felt he wasn't pulling his weight.

At first, I was going to bung this together with shyness, but then I realized that even though they are superficially similar, shyness is different from non-assertive.

Assertiveness is standing up for yourself without being aggressive or rude. Non-assertive people are like the stereotypical Hollywood ugly girl (when Hollywood takes a supermodel and gives her nerd glasses. Because in Hollywood, there are no ugly people. Only beautiful people and beautiful people with nerd glasses). So your stereotypical heroine, especially in romance movies, always lets everyone push her over till she meets the man of her dreams, who teaches her self-respect, usually by bullying and humiliating her. Hey, whatever works.

Hollywood sometimes uses non-assertive men as well. In their case, they go from super meek to super aggressive. They will end up acting like bullies, humiliating people, but the movie will seem to imply that it's a good thing because the victims deserved it, as they were mean to the hero. Let that sink in: If someone is mean to you, you have the right to commit first degree assault on them. That's Hollywood's lesson, by the way, not mine.

In real life, people who act like this are quickly thrown in society's trash can. People who can't find jobs, their family won't talk to them, people cross the street to avoid them. They are the lepers of modern society. If you are wondering why I am telling you this, it's because Hollywood has conditioned you to believe that aggressiveness is the opposite of shyness. **It is not.** Assertiveness is the opposite of shyness.

Note, now, that assertive is different from aggressive. Assertive is standing up for yourself, without attacking or abusing the other person. This point is very important, as many people assume assertive means picking a fight when someone hurts your feelings. It couldn't be more wrong. If someone cuts off your car, and you give them the finger, or pull up and abuse them, that is not assertive.

Sometimes, being assertive means walking away. I was at the airport, and a passenger was screaming at the girl behind the counter for something that was clearly not her fault. She said, "You know what? I don't have to take this," and left. That was being assertive.

Let me give you another example of assertive versus aggressive, taken from a self-defence view point.

It's late night, and you see a drunken person walking on your lawn. You worry they might vandalise something, and go out to confront them.

Assertive: "Hey mate, you look lost. You feeling okay? Want me to call a taxi for you?"

Not only are you not abusing the person, you are giving them a face-saving exit. This is very important when dealing with angry people, even at work. Sometimes, you might have to swallow your pride to give the other person a face-saving exit. The old adage of win the battle but lose the war comes to mind. Real life is not like a school yard. You don't get to show anyone you are boss. You might humiliate someone today and get away with it, but they will remember it for years. Ask yourself: Is it worth it?

And now, the aggressive response: "Hey you! Get the hell off my lawn before I beat the crap out of you."

If you think this example is exaggerated, this is the true story of many people in prison, or buried underground. There have been many cases of people chasing intruders from their houses, following them to the street, and beating the crap out of them. And when the police turn up, they claim they were only defending themselves.

Assertiveness also comes in handy when you feel someone insulted you. The Internet is full of people claiming how evil their bosses are. It looks like everyone online is suffering from acute paranoia, where the whole world is out to get them. Everyone is willing to go to war over the smallest comment they don't like.

If you feel someone insulted you, step back and think carefully. It is entirely possible the other person made what they thought was a harmless comment. The excellent Marc McYoung has this to say:

"When something someone said hurts you, learn to ask 'Excuse me, but when you said that, what did you mean...?'

Instead of assuming that the person intentionally meant to inflict emotional distress on you, check to see what is going on. It is amazing how often you will find that a comment that you found hurtful wasn't meant as such. By asking what the person meant instead of accusing them of what you thought they meant ('Are you saying that I'm ...') you are not only giving the person a chance to explain, but you are keeping yourself from wrongfully attacking.

It is worth the time and effort to find out what is really going on; this instead of reacting emotionally and striking back at the person who you feel hurt you. The reason the latter strategy doesn't work very well is to that person's perception, you're the one who suddenly got vicious and mean. He didn't say anything hurtful, YOU DID! See how easily this can lead to two people both believing that they are defending themselves against unwarranted attacks?"

http://www.nononsenseselfdefense.com/assertiveness.html

A good distinction to make is between a criticism and a complaint. A criticism is a personal attack that accomplishes nothing but pisses the other person off. "You are such a lazy worker. If you want something done, do it yourself."

A complaint addresses an immediate, fixable problem. It can be, and should be, addressed in the now. A criticism is a legitimate complaint that has turned into an attack, and instead of fixing a problem, it becomes an ego match.

It's very important to deal with any lingering issues promptly. It's better to have a small confrontation now, rather than a huge screaming fight six weeks from now.

Justin Jackson goes one step ahead and says that it's healthy to have small confrontations regularly, preventing any simmering issues from blowing up. He gives a few tips on how to have a: healthy confrontation

"Deal with issues immediately, as they arise: letting emotions fester is dangerous. As quickly as you can, respond

to the issue.

Do it in-person: a healthy confrontation occurs in-person, or on the phone. There's something humanizing about speaking to someone, hearing their voice, and seeing their body language.

Be calm, respectful, and direct: address your teammate with respect and grace, but clearly address the problem: "I wanted to meet with you to talk about [issue]. I'm hoping we can [resolve the issue / understand each other better / forgive each other]."

Find the root cause: what was the underlying issue? Is there confusion about the company's direction? Was there a lack of training? Is there an individual that doesn't fit your team's culture? Is everyone stressed and grumpy because of a missed deadline?"

http://teambits.io/why-confrontation-is-essential/

So how do you make sure your shyness and non-assertiveness isn't holding you back?

Luckily, I found that there are some easy ways you can counter your natural instinct to hide every time the boss comes around.

First, say hello to everyone. Be nice. Women are naturally good at this. Men struggle, though I suspect this is more of a cultural thing. Men are trained since childhood to be macho and aloof. The cool cowboy don't have time for all this girl talk. He shoots and leaves.

Problem is, in real life, you are not fighting a horde of zombies, where the only way to survive is to kill or be killed. By the way, I read a Cracked.com article that made a good point. It said the reason zombie survival movies, books, and games are so popular is because they give us a fantasy where all the normal social rules no longer apply and you can be as rude, as much of a jerk as possible without having to face any consequences.

In the real world, there are consequences. The problem is, we are trained to be macho and aloof (men especially, but women as well), but that counts against us, as you don't come across as macho but arrogant. Think about that when you see someone you feel is arrogant around you. Are they really rude, or are they trying to cover up their fear by acting macho, the way Hollywood taught them?

The simplest way is just to smile and

say hello to everyone. Be genuinely nice to everyone, even people you don't like, and you will see their attitude change.

To increase your assertiveness, stop being the passive victim at work. You are not a victim stuck in a fantasy, and your boss isn't the villain sent to torment you. If you are in a meeting with your boss or the team, take an active part. Share your opinions. If you are worried about looking stupid, spend five minutes before the meeting thinking about what you are going to say, and make notes. Volunteer to look at difficult problems (but always on company time). Act like you are a active participant in your own career, and not a helpless victim of destiny.

The drama queen

Many people see themselves as heroes of their own fantasy. They think the whole world revolves around them, that they are stars of their own reality show. If you have ever used these words: "Why does it always happen to me," then you are a drama queen, too.

In the world of drama queens, everything that happens to them is part of a great conspiracy. If the boss doesn't answer your email, it's not because he is swamped. It's because he hates you.

If your co-workers are constantly calling you lazy, it's not because you are, but because they are jealous of you.

Each one of us has a drama queen element in us.

You are an active participant in your own future. Stop acting like some invisible force of destiny controls you.

Hammy went to see Bob. "Hey Bob, you made a mistake in your file. You forgot to include the latest results."

Bob looked at him with a pained face, and Hammy wondered what was wrong. "You guys are always after me! No matter what I do, you find a reason to find fault. Maybe I should just give up. It's obvious nothing I do matters."

While you may find the above example comical, remember the world seems a lot different when you switch places with someone. While you may see yourself as the victim of bullying managers and colleagues, they may see you as a whining drama queen. And you may both be right. As the saying goes, there are multiple versions to each story: Your version, their version, a third party's version, and the truth.

So what can you do? Should you accept bullying just because you don't want to be seen as a drama queen? My advice is to remain calm and focused in all situations and ask for clarification, like the quote from Marc in the last section.

Passive-aggressiveness

I have already said how being overly aggressive is the wrong way to go about things, no matter how satisfying it feels.

Out of all the flaws you can have, passive aggressiveness is the worst, and yet it is the one that is most common. We have been trained to be polite at all times, which in practice comes out as suppressing our anger. This leads to the anger coming out in different ways. From employees who deliberately take it out on customers, so that the customers will never return, to people who carry out minor acts of disobedience, focused on harming the company in small ways. This is the *death by a thousand small cuts* theory. If you can't kill the person with one blow of the sword, give them a thousand small cuts and they will bleed to death. Passive-aggressiveness is the most dangerous things for modern organizations, and for your career, too.

Why do I say that? Because passive-aggressiveness is like threatening to commit suicide if the other person doesn't do what you tell them to. While that may teach the other person a lesson, it causes more harm to yourself. You are killing yourself to make a point.

This is the most dangerous dark pattern. It will not only ruin your career, but your personal life as well. Passive-aggressive (called PA from now) is the last stage for the dark patterns above. If shy people and whiners feel they are constantly ignored, they turn PA. They stop caring, become depressed, and hostile to everything.

How does PA manifest? Employees being deliberately rude to customers, to force them to go elsewhere. Doing shoddy work and hiding it. Breaking small rules, dragging their feet are just a few ways passive-aggressiveness manifests. In places where PA is common, the boss shares the blame too, but if you see yourself going PA, do yourself a favour: Quit. You aren't just hurting the company, you are hurting yourself, too.

PA people are the most dangerous

employees, as unlike bullies, they are not actually abusing anyone, and no one can accuse them of doing anything wrong. But PA people are the ones who are the most harmful to the organization, as they act by stealth. They will not directly do anything to harm the group but will deliberately drag their heels till the morale and output of the whole team suffers.

If you are a manager, PA is the one thing you need to urgently fix. If you are an employee, you need to fix your attitude because it is more harmful to you than to anyone else.

So how do you know if you are PA? The biggest test is "Fuck if I care." If you ever feel like that in a job, in a relationship, anywhere, get out now. Life is too short to do things you don't care about.

PA is the last stage for those who hate their jobs. Please, please, please try to avoid this stage. If you ever start feeling like that, change your thoughts or your job immediately.

Because if you don't, you will turn into one of these nasty people we will talk about next.

Dealing with nasty people

If you have understood the previous few chapters, you will now understand why people act nasty. It is brought about by a feeling of powerlessness and passive-aggressiveness. I will show a few main ways this aggressiveness occurs, and how you can deal with it. Ultimately, you will have to trust your own gut and instincts, but hopefully you will pick up some tips.

1. The Dragon

Summary: The dragon is a very aggressive and direct person. He is the stereotypical bully.

Hammy was walking down to the accounts dungeon, when he felt a breath of hot and stale air. And before he knew it, the Dragon was standing before him.

"Hammy," the Dragon bellowed, "Where be the report thy were to send me?"

Hammy moved back in terror. "I... I... I was... busy..."

The Dragon smelled his fear and moved forward. "Hammy, my boy, this won't do."

The Dragon wants immediate attention. He will threaten and abuse you if you try to ignore him. The more you try to hide, the more aggressive the dragon will get.

The Dragon only wants one thing: To do things his way. If you get in the way, you will be crushed. And it will your fault.

How to fight the dragon— Actually, the dragon is the easiest to fight. As long as he doesn't go into verbal abuse or outright bullying, the dragon can be managed.

Dragons have a very controlling nature. They want to be on top at all times. Have you ever seen people who snivel and make excuses? Perhaps from your school/college days? Well, that's how the dragon sees you. The more you try to hide from them, they more they think you're a slacker, and the harder they will come after you. It doesn't help that many dragons have imposing bodies as well. One dragon I knew was six foot two, and really heavy. And he always cornered you on the stair corners. So what do you do to fight a dragon?

Stand your ground. While you might be terrified, stay calm. The dragon will sense fear and really move in for the kill.

Talk to the dragon logically. This will show the dragon you are in control.

If the dragon makes an unreasonable request, say so. If you stand your ground and explain your position, the dragon will leave you and find someone else to scare.

Cultural issues: The problem is that many people who see themselves as friendly may come across as dragons in a different culture. Different countries and cultures have different rules on how direct you can be. So be careful of judging others, as you maybe seen as the dragon by people under you.

Hammy suddenly straightened himself. "Sorry, Sir Dragon. I was distracted by the new sales presentation."

"I want the report by five p.m. today." The Dragon moved in closer, to scare Hammy. But Hammy stood his ground.

"Sorry, sir, but I have to finish another report. But you will certainly have it by lunch tomorrow."

The Dragon stared at him for a few seconds, and Hammy wondered if he was going to be eaten. But then the Dragon turned away. "Very well. I'll expect your report by lunch. Let's hope you do a good job."

How to avoid becoming one

It is very easy to be seen as the bully once you reach a position of power. If your colleague points out a mistake in your work, you will take the comment happily. If a boss does the same thing, suddenly, you become all defensive. This is the reason many people avoid going into management. Suddenly, they become the bad guys and everything they say or do is seen with suspicion.

So how do you avoid this situation? If you are the boss, you need to be extra careful of how you act.

Even if you aren't the boss, you may still be seen as a dragon in a foreign culture. Many Americans in Japan (and China as well, from what I've heard) come across as loud and abrasive. What counts as normal discussion in America comes across as rude in a different culture. Again, all these things are easy to research. If you are going overseas, talk to expats and get their opinion.

2. The Ninja

Summary: The ninja is someone

who will avoid direct confrontation, choosing instead to attack you by stealth.

While most people are scared of dragons, I think the ninja is more dangerous. What's a ninja?

Hammy finished his presentation. "And that's how, by using a proper testing rig, we will save ourselves a lot of time fixing bugs in the field."

Down the row, the Bob smirked. "Yeah, Hammy. You sure know about fixing bugs, don't you? I guess you are the expert."

Hammy looked at him in frustration. This was the third time Bob had made fun of him.

Ninjas will surprise attack you, embarrass you when you are the weakest, and try to put you down. If you complain, they'll just laugh it off. "Just kidding, old boy. Don't take it so seriously."

The jibes and insults can really bring you down.

How to fight the Ninja? Learn from the best: schoolteachers. They often have to deal with this type of behaviour from students. So what do you do?

Ninjas work by hiding in the

shadows. Bring them out into the open. If a ninja makes fun of you, don't allow them to move on. If you are in a meeting, stop the meeting and ask them to explain. Don't move on until they do.

If ninjas try to hide, you may need to become the dragon. Dragons and ninjas are enemies, as one believes in open attack, the other in a cowardly backstabbing. Corner the ninja and refuse to back down until s/he comes clear. Be polite, as you don't want to be seen as a bully.

Hammy looked at Bob.

"What do you mean by that, Bob? That I cause the most bugs?"

"Well, I do remember your name had the most bugs on the list. But that's not important. Let's move on."

Hammy killed the PowerPoint presentation. "No, Bob, let's not. I'd like to find out what's bothering you, so we can find a solution."

"It's nothing important. Let it go."

"No Bob. If I remember correctly, out of the three critical bugs, two were assigned to you. Is that not correct?"

Bob is sweating by now. "But you

had more bugs than all of us."

"That's because I was working with integrating the code with the other team. This throws up a lot of bugs. Would you like to do this job in the future?"

Bob wipes his sweat. "Ummm."

Kevin the product manager steps forward. "I think what Hammy is saying is we need better testing procedures rather than blaming each other. Continue with your presentation, Hammy."

Bob shakes his head in agreement. "Yes. Let's form a task team to find the best way to integrate with other teams."

How to avoid becoming a ninja: By now, you should be aware that this behaviour is a form of passive-aggressiveness, mixed with non-assertiveness. If you have a problem with someone, talk to them openly. Don't try to sabotage them.

3. The Whiner

Summary: We all know what a whiner is.

Hammy was trying to finish his work when he saw Alec walking towards him. He cursed mentally. The whole day would be wasted now. And he turned out to be right.

"Hammy, the server is down again."

"Sorry Alec, but IT maintain the servers. I just code on them."

"But why does nothing work?"

"Well, IT did say they were doing some rewiring, and we might have a few connection losses."

"But this is wrong! Nothing in this company works. You want to do work, but the servers never work. Even if they were online, our computers are too slow. They take forty-five minutes to compile. And then we get a cryptic error, which takes another hour to debug. And then if you go for a coffee, you find the machine is broken."

Hammy looked at Alec, wondering what he expected him to do. It's clear he expected Hammy to fix this.

"We should fix this. Someone should take initiative and fix this properly. We are a multi-billion dollar company. I can't believe we waste hours just standing around, waiting for the code to compile or the servers to come online. Blah blah blah."

Hammy felt his eyelids going heavy. He suppressed a yawn.

Like dragons, Whiners also like to be in control. But they lack the courage, and feel helpless all the time. So they whine and complain to anyone who will listen.

The problem with whining is it gets irritating real soon. Even if the whiner has some really good points, they get ignored in all the other garbage. If the whiner does make a suggestion that will save the company millions, it will be ignored like everything else s/he says.

While it will usually be your co-workers who will be the whiners, sometimes even bosses turn into them. This is usually the worst combination, as a boss who feels helpless is the worst person to make decisions. Trust me, they'll make you yearn for a bullying dragon.

My father had a boss who was a whiner. My father's chair was broken, and he went to see his boss to have it replaced. The boss started whining. "What can I do? My own table is broken. But no one fixes it. I have been working on a broken table for the last two weeks."

Father said that since he had the control of the budget, why didn't he just call someone to fix it? But all he got was more whining. My father then had to go to the bosses' boss to get the chair fixed.

How to fight the Whiner: The first thing is, don't agree with them or get them to explain. Because once a whiner starts, there's no stopping him. Focus on the key points, but whatever you do, don't get sucked into the whiner's world.

Interrupt the whiner by calling his name repeatedly, if necessary. Then force them to focus on the one problem that is the most critical. If the whiner won't focus, you may have to ask them (politely) to leave. But it shouldn't come to that. Get the whiner to focus on one main problem and fix that.

Alec had been going on for minutes when Hammy decided to intervene.

"Alec. Alec. Alec. Stop talking."

Alec stopped, surprised to hear his name being repeated.

"What is the main problem?" asked Hammy.

"Nothing works in this company. I have been trying..."

"Alec. Alec. What's the main problem?"

"I can't compile my code! I have to

check my code in by five, or I'll be in trouble. We are doing a customer build today, and I can't test anything, because I can't compile it! My PC runs Windows, but the code only compiles on Linux. And the Linux server is down."

"I see. I have a virtual machine copy of the server. Will that do?"

For the first time, Alec smiled. "Perfect. That'll really help."

And Alec left, leaving Hammy alone to finish his own work.

How to avoid becoming one: If your goal is to fix problems rather than complain about them, you will never become a whiner. Whiners feel powerless and use drama queen tactics to deal with problems rather than being assertive.

4. The Gandalf

Summary: The Gandalf will refuse to help you, stonewall and/or ignore you completely. You have seen that scene in The Lord of the Rings, haven't you?

Hammy went to see Matt, the product manager.

"Matt, last year you looked at the Linux server problem. Can I see your results

please?"

"No."

"No?"

"No. It's not gonna work. Trust me. You are better off trying something else."

Hammy walked away frustrated. He would have preferred if Matt had let him decide if the results were useless.

Gandalfs are known for one main thing: saying no to everything. Their only job is to slow you and frustrate you.

Gandalfs are frustrated with life, and negativity and fear avoidance seem to be their only guiding principles. It can be very irritating dealing with them.

How to fight a Gandalf: There are two possible ways.

Bureaucracy can actually help you here. Email everyone involved with a simple message: "I can't finish my work unless ABC gives me what I need." Be warned that this might lead to bad blood.

A slightly better way is to work with the Gandalf. Their negativity is born from hard experience and failure. Rather than pick a fight, you could try and work around them. Or, you could use their negative experience as a learning guide on what to avoid. Perhaps even using the negative person as a mentor. It will require patience, but it's a win-win situation

Hammy went to see Matt again. "Matt, I'm really stuck. I have to see your report."

"I told you, it won't help you."

"That's fine. I'll see it anyway."

"It'll confuse you."

"That's fine. I'm really stuck, and I need to show some progress."

Matt stops his work. "How about this. Meet me in the canteen in fifteen minutes. I'll summarize what I did, and why it won't help you. And then you can decide how you want to proceed. How's that?"

Hammy nodded. "Thanks Matt. See you in a bit."

How to avoid becoming one: Gandalfs are like whiners: passive-aggressive victims of fate. While the whiner will tell everyone how miserable he is, the Gandalf will refuse to do anything. Gandalfs are the height of passive-aggressiveness. So avoid becoming passive-aggressive.

The only thing worse than them is…

5. The Bomb

Summary: The bomb is full of suppressed anger at real or perceived injustices and will explode at the slightest excuse

Hammy went to see T Bomb. "Say Mr T Bomb, I noticed your server crashed last night. What happened?"

As soon as he said it, he regretted it. Something was wrong because T Bomb was staring at him. Hammy could hear the clock in the background ticking down slowly. And then T Bomb exploded.

"Why does everyone always blame me? What do I care? I asked for a new server, but no one cares. It's always my fault. I work with a bunch of fuckin' cheapskates, and I'm the one who gets blamed."

Hammy felt terrified and tried to move back, but T Bomb was having none of that.

"And you. You fucking little kids, right out of university. You think you can teach me my job?"

The Bomb is someone who has a lot of suppressed anger. They have been suppressing it for years, and it all comes out on the wrong person.

How do you deal with the bomb? You don't. If you have a HR department, you get them to deal with it. If you don't, you talk to the boss. Remember, the bomb's problems are not yours to fix, and even though they may have exploded on you, you are nothing but collateral damage. It's the company's job to deal with bombs.

As a short-term solution, you could pretend to be sympathetic with them, but that won't really work, as the bomb will find another excuse to explode another time. My only advice is, stay calm, document everything, and get someone else (hopefully, a manager) to deal with the bomb.

One thing to keep in mind: We all face stressful situations now and then, and maybe the person swearing at you is just having a bad day. Give them the benefit of a doubt. Only if this becomes a pattern, such that many people are scared of talking to this one person, is when you need to get someone else involved.

How to avoid becoming one:
Simple. If you follow everything I've said until now, you should never reach this stage.

Things you need to start doing

Okay. We have talked enough about what you need to stop doing, what you need to avoid. Now we need to talk about what you actually need to start doing. One of the best things to learn is how to communicate well.

Communication is the most important thing you can learn. People earn trust based on how well they communicate what they do, not how well they do it. Your boss doesn't have time to check on everything and everyone. It's your job to manage your own career, not anyone else's. It's your job to communicate what you have done in a clear manner.

A related thing is trust. People are promoted based on how well their manager trusts them not to embarrass him, and not based on talent. Your job is to make your boss look good. Don't get all cynical on me. Don't complain the game is fixed or corrupt. The game is the way it is. You choose if you want to play it. The best way to rise in the corporate world is to be seen doing impressive things. Peoples' impression of you matters. I'm not saying go around stealing other people's work; I'm saying make sure everyone knows what you did and how it helped the company.

You may be the best employee in the world, but if your bosses aren't aware of your accomplishments, your work is worth nothing. But this isn't just about impressing your boss. If you ever want to break out on your own and run your own gig, you need to learn how to communicate. We'll come back to this later.

Taking responsibility

One way to rise above the level of a hamster is to start taking responsibility. A clear sign of being a hamster is that you only do what you are told. If you are only doing what you are told to, then no matter how good you are, you will always be stuck at the level of an employee, a plain old hamster. And the hamster is never promoted.

Not only that, even if you strike out on your own, you will still struggle, as you haven't learnt the skills that make you useful. While it is fun to bash the political games of the corporate world, and I have done so many times myself, you have to understand that there is a reason the corporate world is the way it is. "Investors" (who are, as I have previously said, pure gamblers) pressure CEOs to make a quick profit at the expense of everything. The CEOs pressure their underlings till down the chain, your boss bullies you. And then you have these weird things called customers, who in theory would be number one, but in practice are below the shareholders and the CEO's dog (as we all know, customers have to wait while Fluffy is getting a haircut).

Anyway, coming back on track. All managers are under (sometimes) intense pressure to meet unreasonable goals set by people who have no skin in the game. Like druggies, the "investors" want a quick fix and don't care who has to suffer for them to get it.

In this environment, is it any surprise that anything works at all?

One way to rise above hamster level is to start taking initiative. Understand that there is more to any problem than what the boss just says. Everything you are asked to do is a part of a big picture. Try to understand the big picture, and see how you can do more than the bare minimum. Volunteer to do more than asked.

Before we go ahead, let me answer a possible criticism in your mind. "But Shantnu, if I start volunteering for more stuff, I'll be forced to do a lot of overtime. I'm already staying late. Don't want to do more overtime!"

The first thing is, who is asking you to do overtime? What I'm saying is every time you are asked to do a project, don't just run off to your cubicle and do it. Look at the big picture and see what you can do better. Then talk to your boss, and see if s/he agrees. If they think it's useful, offer to look at the problem on company time. If your boss expects you to look at company problems on personal time, it's time for a new job.

If you have a suggestion that can save the company time, money, or resources, chances are very high that your boss will ask you to look at it. Even if the idea isn't accepted, you will still come across as someone who is proactively trying to help the company. As I have said, promotions depend on impressions. If your managers has the impression that you are dependable —and more importantly, that you will make them look good—you have a higher chance of promotion.

Conversely, if your managers have a bad impression of you or don't even know you exist, you will get no recognition even if you do something that saves the company millions. Ask me how I know.

What if you find there is nothing you can do? Don't worry, you don't have to be an eager puppy, always jumping at your boss' heels. Keep your eyes open, and every time you see something that could be done better, speak up. As I said earlier, you need to be assertive and let your voice be heard.

What if you find something that could help the company, like a new tool, but that won't help the current project? This is quite common. Most companies will know they are not doing everything as efficiently as they can, but they are too snowed under to do anything about it. In such a case, volunteer to look at the new tool. Offer to spend a few hours a week trying it out, on company time, of course. If the tool is useful, your boss might be able to justify your time to his own boss, and you might be given more time to look at it. This is how you slowly build an impression of a dependable person.

But none of this will happen if you keep your mouth shut and stay in your cubicle. The default response of most people to new challenges is to keep their head down. They hope that by keeping quiet, someone else will pick up the problem, and then it'll be their problem. The only problem is that if it's a big enough problem, some manager will be stuck with it, with no knowledge or experience of how to handle it. If you stick your head out of your cubicle for two seconds and volunteer to look at it, you will be saving a your manager a lot of hassle, not to mention doing a lot of good to your career.

I know it's a very clichéd word, but you really need to be proactive. To be really trusted, you need to be in a position where you are never given work. You already know what is happening and what you can do next to help the company. Remember when I was talking about tribes? Your organization is also a tribe, facing its own dangers. These could be other tribes (business rivals), predators (aggressive hedge fund managers who want to forcefully take over your company, fire all the employees, claim a profit, and then flip the company), or natural and environmental disasters (inflation, government policy). But it's worse than that. The tribe is fighting a cancer, the cancer of quick profit and excessive compensation at the C-suite level. So the question is how do you help this tribe? What do you do that can help the tribe fight off predators and rival tribes? If your only answer is, "I will gather some food," or any other such routine activity, then the tribe will take care of you (pay you), as you are helping it in some way, but don't expect anything more than a pat on the back, maybe not even that.

On the other hand, if you keep an eye open and warn the leader when an enemy tribe is getting closer (a competitor has created a product similar to yours and competing directly with you), or when the weather is changing (the government changed some policy that will affect you adversely), then not only will the tribe take care of you but reward you by giving you more power over others. Because remember this if you forget everything else: The tribe takes care of those who help protect the tribe. If your actions directly help the tribe (and you are seen as helping the tribe), the tribe will go out of its way to reward you.

This thinking is also important when you strike out on your own, as I hope you will (since you will always be limited as long as you work for the corporate world). This thinking pattern, that you to have to think of helping others before yourself, will really give you a boost. Even if you start your own business, you have to learn to think like your customer. What do they want, what makes them money? And not how can I squeeze the most pennies out of my few clients?

Lies Hollywood told you, Part 2

One of the most dangerous and stupid ideas that Hollywood has spread, the one that has caused the most harm, is the idea of the *good guy*. And it's always a guy, never a gal. The Hollywood good guy is usually a jerk, treats women like sex objects (because he expects the hot woman to go out with him just because he is the good guy), is a hypocrite (engages in the same behaviour he chides the bad guy for), and has almost no redeeming qualities except that in his own eyes, he is the good guy. This leads to the situation where people who spend all their free time watching TV or playing video games expect to get the top jobs or promotions because in their own eyes, they are the good guys. The thinking goes like, "Hey, I am not a racist, I don't beat my girlfriend, I don't shoplift, which means I'm such a good person. I deserve everything that's coming to me. Now I just need a bigger garage to park my BMW."

And before you think I'm judging you, the above was my exact thought. I used to think like that—"I'm such a nice guy. I gave two dollars to charity, so little Hamad in Africa can buy a goat and live like a king by selling the goat's milk. I'm sure to be rewarded by the Universal Reward System by getting a million-dollar-a-year job, not to mention a racing car and supermodel wife."

It's not enough to think about being a good person or to not have any negative qualities. The world judges you by your output. So if you claim you are a great programmer, what do you have to show for it? You don't need to have written your own operating system; even a small blog that shows a tiny project you built is good enough.

If you claim to be a top graphic artist, what do you have to show for it? Again, you don't need your own web comic that gets twenty million visits a month. A few drawings on DeviantArt that you can point to and say, "This is what I can do."

If you claim you are a kind person, what do you have to show for it? No, that two-dollar donation to buy a goat for Hamad doesn't count.

The tribe lives by a simple rule: We will judge you by what you produce. We only care about what you have done for the tribe, not what a good person you are inside.

Many people here will assume that you need to be a top programmer/artists/author/whatever to succeed. "But how can I compete with all those big multi-million dollar enterprises? Who is going to notice my little Github project, my little painting, or my little book?"

To which the first answer is: you are not competing with the multi-million-dollar enterprises. They are competing with other multi-million-dollar groups.

The second problem is bigger, and the reason you don't do anything. "Who will care about this tiny thing I made? Why even bother?"

But is that really a creation problem or an ego problem? Most people expect fame and fortune with the very first thing they create. They write a novel and expect it to be a New York Times bestseller in a few weeks. If they write a short computer program, they expect to be featured on the front page of Hacker News or Reddit, with a million visits to their website. If they create a painting/graphic, they expect Disney to be knocking on their door within weeks. If not

Disney, at least a Japanese studio (but not the ones that produce tentacle anime, which I've never seen or heard of, because I am a good little boy).

Many people start blogs. Many people call themselves writers. They are working on this great book. It'll be the next great American novel.

Problem is, they've been working on it for years. I know one woman who has been writing a novel for seven years. The arty farty English literature professor types love this thinking. According to them, writing is a divine inspiration that comes from the heavens above, and no mortal can hope to just write stuff.

But do you think Shakespeare, with his dozens of plays, sat there on his butt, waiting for some inspiration to fall on his head? Shakespeare, Dickens, Jane Austen, all the writers the English professors love, they weren't writing to impress some English teacher. They were writing to put food on the table.

Do a quick experiment. Look up your favourite writer. Go to their Wikipedia page and see how many books they wrote.

Charles Dickens is known for *A*

Christmas Carol and *Oliver Twist*, but he wrote more than fifteen novels and dozens and dozens of short stories.

One of my favourite novelists is Issac Asimov, of the *Three Laws of Robotics* fame. He wrote more than five hundred books and stories. Yes, you read that right. If you look at his bibliography page on Wikipedia , they have alphabetical sections to go through all the work he wrote.

So what's the point? All these people started in complete obscurity. If you look at famous writers, or bloggers, or artists, they usually have dozens, if not hundreds, of works before the one they become famous for. That's where the concept of the overnight success comes from. "After ten years of struggle, I became an overnight success" says the cynic.

And this is the problem with many people unhappy with their lives. They never start anything. They dream of doing great things. They have grand plans. Plans that will end in million-dollar books, business ideas that will be making millions in six months, code that will end up being used by Google and everyone else on the planet. But they never start with their ideas. They never actually build anything. Ideas are cheap. I can give you ten ideas for bestselling novels or million-dollar businesses right now. But how will that help you? Unless you go out and actually build something, ideas are useless.

The tribe is under constant danger. What do you have to show for your talents? Whatever you do doesn't have to make money, but it does have to be useful to the tribe. What have you done in the last week that helped your fellow human beings?

You are not the Chosen One

Earlier, we talked about how Hollywood has conditioned you to believe that you are the hero of your story. That you will find a strange alien/foreign mentor who will teach you The Secret of Success (TM). He will teach you the real secret, the one the rich people have, yours for only six payments of $99.99. (Actually, I can do that as well. Contact me offline. I'll give you the Super Duper Secret of Success).

In real life, no magical foreigner/alien/wizard will come and teach you how to excel in life. You'll have to learn to do it yourself. Chances are, it will take years, though once it does happen, people will dismiss you as a lucky overnight success.

So how does one become a success? Look at navy captains. They spend years studying battle tactics, electronics, communications, and a hundred other subjects before they even come close to being considered for command.

Look at Issac Asimov with his five hundred works, banging out story after story after story.

Look at David Wong of Cracked.com, who wrote stories on his website for thirteen years before he got a bestseller.

These people found something they loved and continued doing it over and over again.

You are not the chosen one

And that is a good thing. Because you are not the victim of some destiny or prophesy or fate. You control your own life and your own happiness.

Escape the cubicle

To ever rise above the level of the hamster, you need to learn the skills of business. These skills are not just necessary to work for Da Man, but also if you ever want to work for yourself.

There are many ways to escape the cubicle, some of which include rising in management till you become a C-suite executive; however, I won't go into those. Simple personal bias. I can't sell you something which I'm not convinced about. Instead, the three main ways that I would recommend are:

1. Become The Expert in a field so that you are the first choice for people struggling with a certain domain, and you can make money by teaching, too.

2. Become a top-tier consultant. The ones that can charge hundreds of dollars an hour and work the hours they want.

3. Start your own business and become your own boss.

Now, all writers show their bias. If I was a completely reasonable person, I would show you the advantages/disadvantages of each, complete with bullet points and dumbed-down tiny paragraphs.

But I'm not.

I'm not a machine or one of these five-dollar-a-page writers. Being reasonable/logical is often a sign of cowardice: The writer is too scared to make a stand and so throws a million options at you, hoping you will make the choice yourself.

I, on the other hand, would like to make a stand. My belief is that the best way to escape Hamster-dom, with its constant futile struggles, its performance reviews designed purely to humiliate you, its non-stop rat race with no winning goal in sight, is to strike out on your own. Do your own thing. Run your own business.

Now, the problem with starting your own thing is that no one has heard of you, so why would they buy from you? When was the last time you bought a book or a video course or a software from some dude you just heard about? Which is why I like Amy Hoy's advice. Start with something small, like an eBook or informational product. That way, you build credibility and show your expertise. From there, you can go into consulting, become the expert, or start your own business. You may find that you end up doing all three of the above. So you may start with a small book, get a few consulting gigs based on that, and then start a software company based on what you learnt. Or you may go straight from a book to a viable business.

But I hope that the end will always be the same: You will be doing your own thing, choosing your own work and hours. And that's when you can say confidently: "Dude, I ain't no hamster no more."

Before you can throw off the shackles of Hamster-dom, you need to learn a bit about business.

You are your own brand

To start off, start treating yourself like a brand, a product. The reason so many people hate their jobs and feel stuck is because they never took initiative in guiding their own fate. Like a leaf in the wind, they flew wherever the market forces took them. But that is a bad way to go if you want to become independent.

The first thing you need to do is increase your visibility. Many people, especially technical types, suffer from an extreme case of social phobia. They never create a blog or any other online account. Or if they do, they will use a name like *stud_muffin_ninja*. Many people are terrified of being recognised by their bosses or colleagues. "What will *they* think?" Everyone is scared of some invisible *them* who will judge them and laugh at them.

Well, let me put your mind at rest. No one is looking at you. In fact, no one cares about you. How much time do you spend Googling your colleagues (even the good-looking ones)? Have you ever looked at the LinkedIn profile for anyone at your work? Do you even have a LinkedIn profile?

Let me tell you the sad truth of life: No one cares about you. I was like that for a long time. I was scared of being recognised. What will the people think? I better be careful about what I write. I better not use my real name, in case *they* find me.

Well, here's what I found. You may write the best blog in the world. You may write a book that shares your ten years' wisdom in some specialised field. You might create the best learning course on a highly in-demand topic.

And no one will care.

Not a single person.

Your blog will get two visitors, one of whom will your mother-in-law posting a message about how impressed she is with you (I never found out who the second person who visited my website was. Probably a ghost).

So why bother? And here we come to the cynical, passive-aggressive attitude I have been talking about. "Nothing matters, so why do anything?"

We will come to that, but before I go ahead, let me convince you one more time. Use your real name and try to build an online profile. No one cares about you. If you have something interesting to say, you will have to grab people by the throat and tell it to them.

Why you must teach

How do you build your brand? By teaching, of course.

"But Shantnu, I am not an expert. How can I teach? *They* will point fingers at me and laugh!"

There you go worrying about *them* again. Who cares what *they* think?

You don't teach because you are an expert. You become an expert by teaching.

When I started writing this book (and the blog posts that inspired it), I wasn't an expert on career coaching or any such thing. But I kept writing because a few people were really touched by what I wrote. I got emails saying, "I wish I knew this X years ago," or "This is exactly how I feel in my job." I also got messages on forums that said basically, "What a waste of time that was. Boring." Which just goes to show you can't please everyone.

If I had tried to become an expert, I would have spent ten years getting a PhD and then several years consulting. But by then, I would have been useless to you, as I would speak like a consultant and have no idea of the problems you face.

Why do I insist you teach? Because we are facing the forces of decay, and the entropy of the system is always increasing. The default state for you is to do nothing. You think about becoming a top expert, a top programmers or designer, yet you go back to watching reruns of *Baywatch*. If you want to escape this state of decay, you need to put in a lot of effort.

And the best effort is to teach something.

"But I'm not an expert!"

No one cares. There are no true experts anywhere in the world. We are all at varying levels of competence. If I am at level nineteen of some art (a made-up number), for example, and you are eighteen, I can teach you, even though we are both amateurs to someone who is a twenty-five.

Teaching (which doesn't have to be formal teaching by the way; it can be simple blog posts) forces you to think critically about what you are doing. It forces you to communicate your thoughts in a clear and coherent manner. What's the number one skill in the world? Communication. The people most successful are not those who are technically the best, but those who are best at communicating their vision.

You might be the best programmer in the world. But if all you do is hide in your cubicle, no one will know. You might be the best writer in the world, but if you never publish anything, no one will hear of you. You might be the best artist in the world, but if you hide your painting in your toilet, no one will care (except for those unlucky enough to get a bad tummy in your house).

Most people spend years developing their skills but spend no time in learning how to market themselves. In the real world, how competent you are is only half the story. The other half is: how do other people view you? And not just your bosses, but your colleagues, the wider community you are a part of and the general population you serve.

Your skill is useless without visibility. That's the reason you don't get any respect at work. While you think you are doing a great job, others don't think so. The largest reason being they aren't aware of it (which itself is caused by them not caring about you. People only care about themselves, remember?)

Let's say your skill level can be measured on a scale of 0 to 100. And so can your visibility.

Let's now say you are the best programmer in the world, but very shy, so no one has heard of you. So you are 100 in programming, but 0 in visibility. So your total impression is: $100 \times 0 = 0$. A big nothing. No one cares about you.

Now let's look at your manager. He

may only have 30 skill, but 50 visibility. So the total for him is: 30 x 50 = 1500.

Now you see why the suits get more respect than you? They have learnt the secret. Being competent is good, but being visible is more important.

Now let's say you spend some time building your skills, but you also learn how to market yourself. Rather than being a one-trick pony, you know a bit about many things. So now you are a 70 in both skill and marketing. So your total impact is:

70 x 70 = 4900.

That blows the 1500 of the barely competent manager out of the water. In fact, since hardly anyone will be a super expert (the ones who score 100), it means that if you have a good mix of technical knowledge as well as the skills to market that knowledge, you will become unbeatable.

Knowledge only has value if you share it with others. So share what you know with others.

Marketing

Right now, at this very moment in time, you have the skills, the knowledge, the hard-earned practical wisdom, to either make someone a lot of money or save them a lot. This person is waiting for someone to solve their problems. S/he is searching through dozens of resumes and not finding anything useful. Or they are trying to use some of these online contract job websites and finding that half the people can't spell their own name, let alone build a website.

How will you reach this person? You have the skills to help them. You have the time, or are willing to make it. That person has gotten very disillusioned after meeting one bad developer after another. How do you convince them that you are the person for them? How do you convince them that you are not wasting their time?

Do you have a really good blog you could point to? Do you have a really good open source project you could show them? "Look, I've solved similar problems before, or written about them in detail. I may be able to help you."

That's all what marketing is. Letting prospective clients/employers know you are in the market, and qualified to help them.

Sales

Let's talk about a very dirty word. It's so dirty, some of you will be shocked.

Others will close the book and never return. You will accuse me of being uncivilised and brutish, and ask me to mind my language. What's this dirty word? Cover your ears, sensitive types.

Sales.

Yes, selling. The dirty, dirty little word. Ouch. Why would I bring in smut like that? After all, you thought this book was family safe, and now I'm talking about sales?

Why does sales get such a bad rep?

It's because most salesmen are selling other people's stuff. They have no interest in the actual product. They are not rewarded for building a long-term relationship with the customer. Instead, they are paid based on how many units of crap they sell. Not only that, they had no input in creating the product—they are brought in at the end, by which time it's too late to guess if the customer even cares about the product.

But you don't have to be like that. Sales are important, not just if you are a salesman or a bootstrapper. Do you want to convince your boss to try a new technology? Some cool new tool that you think will look good on your resume, but which your boss doesn't care about, as it does nothing for his resume. You need to understand sales.

So sales is convincing him that the tool is actually useful for the company as a whole and will add to the bottom line, i.e., will bring in more money than it cost (which may be the cost of installing the tool and training the users, which are real costs if you run a business).

Think about how you would go about doing this. Would you call your boss (or go speak to him) nonstop till he obliged? Would you spam him mercilessly? Would you promise to cure cancer and AIDS, if only he bought the software? Aren't these the things normal salesmen do: Aggressive selling with impossible promises?

Now tell me this: How many times do these tactics work? How many times have they worked with you?

Exactly.

Taking your boss's example, to really convince him to buy that tool for you, you'll have to speak in his terms, using the language that he understands.

"Hey boss, X will look really good on my resume. Can we buy it, please?"

Versus

"Hey boss. Many people are saying that X saves two hours every week. That means for our team, we can save twenty hours a week. We could use that time to add new features and deliver our product early."

Now you are making your boss look good. Even if the tool is out of his budget, you have given him a good bargaining chip to go to his boss and convince her to foot the budget.

Good sales is always a win-win game

That is what all these aggressive pushy salesmen forget. Just because you have to meet some imaginary quota your boss set don't mean I have to buy your crap. What's in it for me?

If you are planning to start a business or something similar, a similar principle applies. What are people looking for? What can you sell them that will help them make their lives easy? Remember, we are looking for a win-win situation. What makes people miserable, and how can you fix their problems? That's all what sales is.

But most people, when they decide to start a blog or build a website or write a book, have no idea what to do. So they resort to the default of spamming people. They see everyone doing it, and a few spammers even making money, so they wonder why they can't do it.

How does this apply if you don't want to start a company?

Well, say you want to get a dream job somewhere you have always wanted to work. For example, a start-up (though never say, 'I will only work for Google.' That way, you will miss other opportunities that may be better than Google).

Look for what industry and type of company you want to work for (start-up, top paying etc). Then look for what skills the employers in these domains are looking for and how you can reach them. Plastering them with your resumes is one way to do it; you will get the same reaction as you would to spam email.

Instead, why don't you write a great series of blogs or a great book on the skills the company is looking for, or create a series of videocasts? So that your potential employer has heard of you before you even apply to them.

The people who get the best jobs are

not the ones who are best at their chosen field. Rather, they are the ones best at selling themselves. Similarly, the person called for the interview is the one with the best resume, not the one who is the most qualified. You need to learn to sell yourself. However, as you have seen, sales is not a dirty word. Always keep this in mind: You are looking for a win-win situation. If you think like that, you do not have to worry about looking sleazy. A fair exchange is no robbery. If someone is looking for your skills and is willing to pay for it, why would you not make the best effort to look good in front of them?

It's a bit like dating. If you are in your thirties or older, you have probably gotten over the "One True Love" formula Hollywood tries to ram down our throats. "When you meet Your One True Love, you will know." Sure. And that's the day you will also find out that you are secretly a wizard and the only person who can stop the evil Lord Evil with your magical skills.

For the rest of us, we have to work with what we have. When you go on a date, do you not spend time trying to look good? What is that if not sales and marketing? You are trying to show your best side forward.

You are trying to show your prospective partner your best qualities, while at the same time judging his/her qualities. If you both find you are suitable for each other, that counts as a closed sale.

As you can imagine, I am a very romantic person.

Branding

You need to have your own personal brand. It can be informal and chatty, like Amy Hoy. It can be formal, or it can be somewhere in between, like Jeff Atwood. But when you start to build an online brand, make sure you focus on one thing and one thing only. So no mixing Apple products with toilets (real life example from Justin Jackson's blog).

You don't need have a brand that is boring and dry; you are not writing for a journal or applying for a teaching post. But it does have to be consistent.

That's why you have to not just share your information, but share it in such a way that it is useful to the tribe. People only care about what you can do for them. If you are not helping the tribe, you don't exist. Simple. That's why I hate the term "Read the Fucking Manual." No, you read the fucking manual. Why is the manual so hard to read? Why do you even have a manual?

It will only make sense if you are thinking of the tribe. How are you helping the tribe? How are you helping other people achieve their goals?

The strangest thing

This thing is so strange that it still doesn't make sense to me. But it is true, and I have seen so with my personal experience, not to mention in the experience of others.

The best way to get others to listen to you is to actually help them first. So don't market yourself, market others. Don't solve your own problems. Solve others' problems. Don't talk about what a great product you built. Listen to what others are struggling with.

The strange thing is that people will pay more attention to you if you just stop talking about yourself for a minute and actually listen to what they have to say.

Surprise, the religions were right about one thing: Helping your fellow men/women is the way to succeed.

Summary

To summarise everything in this

chapter: Find something you are passionate about, something you love and are willing to spend hundreds of hours on. It can be anything, with one caveat: It must be a field people are willing to and able to spend money on. So no targeting college students or schoolteachers. Find something you love and establish your expertise in it. If you can't find a field, choose anything you find interesting, and spend time mastering it. Passion is not like Harry Potter's magic: You aren't born with it. **Learn to grow into your passion.**

The important thing is to start and not waste time over-analysing or causing a paralysis by analysis. Just pick a damn thing. (For comparison, I started my blog to teach the Python programming language. It morphed to programmer advice to general career advice. But none of this would have happened if I had sat on my butt, making grandiose plans).

Once you have chosen a field, start establishing your expertise. Write blogs, create video tutorials, find out how you can genuinely help people. Learn how to sell, how to market and promote. This is why I recommend starting with a tiny product, as you won't spend years building something no one wants to buy. Instead, you build a tiny thing, find how to sell it, build something bigger, find ways to charge for it, and so on. This way, rather than jumping in the middle and getting lost, you are slowly building your business skills, convincing not only others, but more importantly yourself, that you have what it takes to run a good business. When you start off, your income from these projects will be minuscule, but over time, it will grow and grow, till you will be able to quit the day job and do your own stuff. Remember to send me a tip then.

Stop being the hamster

That's it, folks. We must end our journey here.

Let me sum up what I've been trying to say. You've been brought up to become passive and submissive. All your life, you were fed a formula of "Do what you're told, and all will be well."

The problem is the people giving you this advice are working on nineteenth century manufacturing principles. Turning up and doing the work no longer works.

But the main reason you feel depressed is because you feel powerless. You are not in control of your life, and nothing you do seems to matter.

My goal in this book has been to show you that you are not, in fact, helpless. You just have never known what to do. If they won't give you a chance to get ahead, go ahead and grab the damn chance by the neck. What are you waiting for? Permission?

Someone to come and tell you that your idea doesn't suck, and *they* won't laugh at you?

I give you all the permission you need. **I give you permission to be awesome.**

Through my blogs and this book, I may have been giving you the impression that I am an expert. I am not. In fact, I hate the term expert. Experts are people who plant their flags on one side and then refuse to budge, no matter how much evidence you show them.

Even I feel low and sad at times. I feel my life hasn't been going anywhere. I feel jealous when people much younger than me achieve much bigger success. But by now, I have trained my mind to bounce back and focus on the positive. I have found that taking initiative and being proactive is the best way to beat depression. Pick a small project, anything. A small book, a tiny open source project, a blog on anything you love. Make sure it is tiny, or you will never finish it. Finishing a complete project gives great satisfaction and helps you in your journey to escape the cubicle.

Don't worry about making money on your first project. In the beginning, we are trying to raise your profile, to prove that you are credible and professional. Over time (and this is counted in years, not weeks), your reputation will grow. People will begin to trust you. That's the time you can move into your chosen career—whether it is a top tier consultant or an entrepreneur running his/her own company.

But none of that will happen unless you take the first step and actually start something. Most people fail here. They daydream about doing great things one day, but never actually start anything.

Just starting isn't enough, though. You need to finish it as well. And that's the second place most people fail. They start something with excitement. Every project is exciting in the first few days, like a romantic affair. You can only see the sexy parts, and everything looks hunky dory.

But complete projects are like marriages—you have to work through not just the romantic parts but the boring parts, the parts you hate, the parts where it all seems a drag, the parts where you begin to doubt yourself and wonder if you have made a big mistake, the parts where you want to throw it all away and start again. And you don't get any sex at the end of it, either (because that's what marriage is like).

So how do you go through the bad phases? Find other people like you. Join a group of like-minded people and share your progress with them. You are more likely to succeed if you commit publicly to finishing a project (psychologically speaking). Not only that, you can keep each other honest. Joining a group will also show you that you are not the only one who faces these problems. Everyone struggles, even the ones who have been doing it for years. The only difference is they have learnt to keep going through the good times and the bad.

And that is the only difference between losers and winners. The winners don't know how to quit.

Thank you

Thanks for reading folks.

The blogs that inspired this book

This book was inspired by two blogs I wrote, that got me got me 25,000 views in a few hours and crashed my server. I got so many replies and comments to the blog, that I decided to write a book on the topic.

When I had started writing this book, I had made the decision not to copy-paste from my blog. But the blog posts are still useful, so I will add them to the Appendix.

Note that these are taken from my blog, so they aren't edited in any way. I originally wrote them for a programming blog, but the advice they give is universal.

How to Survive a job you hate

I thought I was in a great place. I was grinding out code like a horny teenager grinds out you know what. If I had been born in the 70s, I would have been walking to Stayin Alive.

And then, I was called into a meeting with a senior manager, almost at vice president level. And he basically told me that I was the lowest performer in the company, because "he hadn't seen my name at all in any of the progress reports." He didn't bother to ask my direct manager, because in the world of senior managers, what isn't written in email reports doesn't exist.

Sort of like the quantum world, where particles only exist when you observe them. You know, Schrodinger's cat and stuff?

So because some middle level manager had forgotten to put my name on email reports, I didn't "exist". If you have read Catch 22, this happens to the doctor. He dies on paper, and the people stop talking to him because he is officially dead, even though he is standing right in front of them.

I joke about it now, but at the time I was quite hurt. I had never felt so humiliated in my life

I thought about quitting, but couldn't because of some legal / finance issues. Basically, the company had sponsored my visa, and if I quit, I'd have to pay them thousands of pounds I didn't have. Besides, for other, personal reasons, I couldn't move city, and there were no jobs in my city.

So I had to swallow my humiliation, and go back to work at a place I felt sick. And I mean this literally. That year, I took something like 7-8 sick periods, each lasting 2-3 days. I was put on an official HR checklist, as even in our relatively relaxed environment, that was too much.

But I survived, and as the cliche goes, what doesn't kill you makes you the President of Azerbijan.

If you too are stuck in a job you can't leave, here are some tips that may help you survive.

Surviving a work place you absolutely hate

Take stock of your life

The first thing to do is take stock of your life. Until then, I had been cruising along in life. I didn't have any savings, even though I was single and living in a cheap house. I wasted my time playing games, and didn't do anything to improve my career. As soon as the incident above happened, I decided to reevaluate my life. This is a very personal process, and will be different for each of us. But take a blank diary, and write down all you feel is wrong with your life. If you don't want to write it down, sit in a quiet place, and just think about it. You won't have to think hard. Your subconscious already knows whats wrong: You just have to acknowledge it. There is no need to take action on this list yet. That will happen automatically when you are ready to move to the next step.

Second, decide what you want to do in life. Do you want to be a top notch contractor, charging hundreds of dollars an hour? Do you want to start your own software company? Get a job at $Big_Company? You don't need to be certain at this stage, and you can even have multiple options. But do think about the details. So if you want to become a startup founder with your own web based business, do you know how to create and run websites? Do you know how to sell on the internet?

Next, start looking at how you can improve your skills. Don't blindly change a job. That's my advice. Because whatever problems you face now, you will carry them to the next job. Changing your environment will not change your situation. There is a reason you are in the mess you are in, and if you just move job, you will end up in the same situation again. So that's why I say, look to improve your skills, so you can move on to something better, not just more of the same crap.

Why you should not quit a job you hate

This will fly against everything you have been told: If you hate your job, quit immediately! Walk in, give the finger to the boss, and storm out. But that will not accomplish anything.

This point is very important. Just changing your job will not improve your life, unless you also change the thinking that got you into this mess. What thinking?

If you think all managers are evil and working for Da Man, you will never take on responsibility. Which means you will never get promoted, no matter how many jobs you change.

If you think capitalism and business is evil, you may never think of selling that app you wrote, and that many people would be willing to pay good money for. You will be stuck blaming evil bankers or foreigners for your problems.

If you think (like 90% of programmers) that being technically good is good enough to get promoted and get pay rises, you should be prepared for a good bitch slap by Real Life. Don't worry, I'll be there to laugh at you, and then pick you up, and welcome you to the club. We all been there, and the sooner you get slapped down by life, the sooner you will be ready to face life as it really is, and not how you want it to be.

If you accept you are responsible for your own life, you must also accept that your current circumstances, the ones you hate so much, are partly (or wholly, depending on how honest you are) your fault. So if you change your job, the bad habits, the wrong thinking patterns that got you into the mess you are, will carry with you to the next job. Changing your environment will not change your circumstances. Read that line again.

Edited to add: Based on comments on Hacker News etc, let me add this:

If you are facing bullying, racism or sexism (or indeed any other -ism), then yes, leave immediately.

But for most of us, it's not outright bullying, but the constant grinding down, the non-stop requests for overtime, the occasional "helpful comments" that are actually insults, the constant interference, that really gets us down. Individually, they might mean nothing, but over time, they build up, and make you feel as small as the full stop at the end of this sentence. If you are facing this constant humiliation, that's when you must plan your exit.

End of edit

So what should you do?

Find out which negative patterns are holding you back from your goals. You may need the help of loved ones, friends, or even a therapist. You can do this by yourself, if you can be brutally honest, but I found it easier to get help, to see my own blind spots. And then, change your thinking (and no, it won't happen overnight). You may find that you no longer hate your job. Or you may find that you are now skilled enough to do better. Either way, you will be in a better position to move forward, than if you had just given the finger and moved on.

Start building your skills

Which skills? You should already have a rough idea of what you want to do. Start with the skills required for that. Luckily, some skills are common. No matter what you do, learning to sell yourself will come in handy. Other than that, you might want to learn things that you find relevant, or even interesting. Don't dismiss interesting, as you more likely to stick with things you love. These might be making a website, learning a new programming language, making professional looking video casts, or even improving your writing.

Start to take control of your life. Most depression is caused by feeling helpless, a victim of fate. If your work won't allow it, trying taking initiative outside. Write a game, build a electromechanical Dalek using Lego and microprocessors, anything that will make you feel good about yourself. Just one thing: Do something that you can finish in a few weeks. Finish, so it is good enough to put online and show to others. Don't choose something like writing the next Lord of the Rings, which will take you 27 years to complete. Choose something from what you want to accomplish, and start making small progress daily.

This point is very important. The reason you are doing this is to build self esteem. Small, regular accomplishments will really build your self esteem.

How to move on to a better job

So how does all this help you?

Simple. You are working on improving your skills in the background, aren't you? Once you feel that you are confident, resign quietly. Don't throw a tantrum, don't give it to them or show them their place. Say "Thanks for everything, but I feel I must move on now." You will come across as very professional, and will certainly get a good reference.

The difference now is that you have built yourself up. You will not just changed one crap job for another. It might take time, but no one said fulfilling your dreams is easy.

Remember that there is a price to pay if you chase after your dreams. But also remember that there will be a bigger price to pay if you crush your dreams and do nothing. You have to pay the price either way, but at least one path leads to happiness.

Dealing with depression

Depression is fairly common amongst people who hate their jobs, or those who feel inadequate. Which, using very simple statistics, is one hundred percent of people. Chances are, you felt depressed at some time in your life. Maybe you overcame it, maybe you still suffer from it. Even if you overcame it, there is a chance it might come back. That is, unless you fix your thinking.

I fought with depression for years, so I'm uniquely qualified to write on this topic. The main thing, the only thing I would say is: While it is normal to feel low now and then, if your depression has continued for weeks or months, see a professional. I know it's hard. You will be judged by people who don't know better. If you tell everyone you have a sexually transmitted disease, the reaction you get will be milder than if you tell them you are suffering from depression. Everyone and his dog will try to "cheer" you up, usually by reading whatever pop psychology book they read. My advice is, see a professional and don't take advice from idiots. Like running marathons, or learning to ride a bicycle, or sex, the only people who can give you advice are those who have actually experienced it.

Choosing a good therapist is a whole book in itself, and it is advice I cannot give here. Feel free to contact me privately. But don't choose the first result you get on Google. Research not only the therapist, but his/her organisation as well. Be sure to avoid ones that use weird new age theories (I once went to a therapist who claimed to use Angelic crystal Reiki to heal people. Don't ask). But also avoid therapists that keep their patients for years in therapy. Such patients become walking ATM machines for the therapist. Most therapists should give you a free consultation. Choose the one who makes you feel the most comfortable.

With that out of the way, there are three main reasons you feel depressed. Only three. Fix them, and in most cases, you will fix your depression.

1. Powerlessness

Most depression is caused by feeling powerless. It's a case of learned helplessness. A mad scientist called Seligman went around electrocuting dogs randomly (and you think your boss sucks)?

And this is what he found:

" In learned helplessness studies, an animal is repeatedly exposed to an aversive stimulus which it cannot escape. Eventually, the animal stops trying to avoid the stimulus and behaves as if it is helpless to change the situation. When opportunities to escape become available, learned helplessness means the animal does not take any action."

[http://en.wikipedia.org/wiki/Learned_helplessness]

The dogs were randomly electrocuted, and later on given a chance to escape. But the dogs had given up, and just kept accepting shocks rather than escaping. They had been trained to become helpless and pathetic.

Why do we do that? Continue accepting pain, rather than leaving? One reason is a feeling of powerlessness. If nothing you do matters, what's the use of doing anything?

That's how the road to hell starts.

How to beat it

The way to beat the feeling of powerlessness is to start taking initiative in life. Try to take more initiative at work. Offer to look at that bug no one will go near. Offer to investigate better code review systems (but always on company time). If your work doesn't allow you take leadership/ownership, start your own project. Do something you own completely. A personal project, but a short one you can finish in a few weeks.

Write a novel, learn a musical instrument, volunteer at a charity. Do anything except watch TV or wasting time on useless websites (except for mine).

2. Self Esteem

You are constantly negative talking to yourself. Everyone does it. "I'm such a loser. What have I done to my life?"

You may be surprised that even people you see as cool and successful do this. I was listening to a talk by a therapist, and he was working with a supermodel. Very attractive, very popular. Yet, when he asked her how she felt about herself, she said:

"I'm a fat, ugly, stupid, red headed bitch."

The therapist knew he had his work cut out then.

And the second lesson from this is that the way we see ourselves may have no basis in reality.

The way we see ourselves is different from how others see us. The problem is, we have been trained to only see the negative in everything we do. Saying you are good at something is considered boasting. Religions teach us to be humble and accept a greater force.

Fixing your self esteem is easy, as all you have to do is start to recognize your achievements, and stop harping on your failures. You will be surprised to know that this process does not take longer than two weeks. Rob Kelly, from whom I stole this technique has treated people who were sexually abused as children, and it took them two weeks to improve their self esteem. So don't tell me it won't work for you, or that you are a special case.

The technique

Get a diary, or use the note feature on your phone. Every day, before going to sleep, write down five things you accomplished. Just five. And they don't even have to be big. Examples:

"We were running out of milk, so I

went and bought it before anyone noticed. At work, I helped a junior engineer fix his code. I remained calm when a customer was abusing me, and helped him fix his problem. I went for a walk/jog after lunch, so that I remain fit."

All small things, things you do everyday, and wouldn't even consider accomplishments. But write them down anyway, at least five points. And read the last few days accomplishments daily as well.

Why does this help?

We don't process our good work, only focussing on the failures. No wonder we feel like shit all the time. By writing down your positive work, you are defeating the self-defeating negative talk, and programming yourself to look at the good things you do. This programming takes no longer than two weeks, but continue it longer if you like it.

In case you didn't understand, let me repeat it. Your brain is like a computer that has been programmed to do this: *for i = 0 to Forever:*

print "I am garbage. I will not accomplish anything in life."

This isn't your fault. No one ever

taught you how to think. It's not your parents fault either, as no one told them either. But now that you know, make sure your children are not programmed to hate themselves.

What you want to do is stop that garbage program, and replace it with a program that processes your accomplishments. That's all what self esteem is.

Absurd Magical Beliefs

One way to feel depressed all the time is to have Absurd Magical Beliefs(AMB). What is an AMB? Things like:

Believing in lucky underwear, lucky color or days

Believing that there is a universal system of justice, call it Karma or anything, that helps the so called "good guys" (you), and punishes the so called "bad guys" (everyone who opposes you).

Belief in astrology, Homeopathy, psychic powers, or anything else not proven by science.

And before you think I'm trying to shove my beliefs down you throat, let me say, I used to believe all this crap myself. I trained as an astrologer, and for a time, I had dozens of people every week asking me for an astrology / psychic reading. And while I was claiming to help them, I was super depressed myself. The more depressed I was, the more the superstitious beliefs I had.

Later on, I found that the two are related.

In case you didn't get the message, let me repeat it: **Belief in superstition is directly related to how depressed you feel. The more depressed you are, the more superstitious you will get.**

Why is that?

Superstition makes you feel powerless. Rather than you being in control of your life, some invisible force of Karma/crystals/ghosts/homeopathy/astrology is controlling you. Since by definition you can't control these forces, that means you end up becoming, at least in your own mind, a helpless victim of fate.

When I say you should accept responsibility for your life, I mean your locus of control. This is a very clear cut and scientific process, with no wooly New Age interpretations. What's the locus of control?

Before that, answer a few questions, in Yes or No.

Warning: If you are not sure, or if the answer is Maybe, write down Yes. Don't play around or try to make excuses. The only acceptable answers are Yes (including maybe/sometimes) and No. Be totally honest with yourself.

1. I am passing a table, when I see the horoscope lying on it. I have a quick look at it. Not that I believe in it, but just for fun.

2. I have a lucky color or underwear or day.

3. I believe that who you know is more important than what you know.

4. I believe the ghosts of people who died are around us.

5. I believe that going to the right University is important, if you want to succeed in life.

6. I believe in past life.

7. I believe in Karma, ie, a Universal system of justice.

8. Alternative medicine systems like Homeopathy are viable alternatives to normal medicine.

9. With all these low cost foreigners entering the market, I can never compete. The future is bleak.

10. It's not easy to become rich. People who become rich have something special in them, an "X" factor, as it were.

11. I believe in conspiracy theories. The world is run by bankers/Jews/Knights Templars/Sponge Bob Squarepants.

The Locus of Control

The locus, if you remember you high school geometry, is the point in a circle (or anywhere else, but circle is good enough for us). Imagine your body is a circle. The locus of control specifies how you view the world:

People with an Internal locus of control believe they are in control of their lives.

People with an external locus believe magical things like astrology, ghosts, or evil bankers and lowly paid foreigners control their life.

Why does it matter? People with an external locus of control are usually the ones always depressed. That's because they believe that magical forces control their life. Like Silegman's dogs, they feel that nothing they do matters, so why bother?

If you answered yes to any of the questions above, your locus of control is external. 1-2 yeses are bad. 4-5 are very bad. More than 5, you need to see a therapist now.

Before you think I'm judging you, I was a score 11 on that chart. I visited astrologers, psychics, crystal therapists, Reiki healers, Angelic Reiki healers (yes, there is such a thing. There is also a Certified Angelic Reiki Healer course. I never understood if it's the angels who come down to Earth to certify the students). But the more psychics I visited, the more depressed I got. That's because I was feeling more and more helpless with each person I visited. I was no longer in control of my life.

The dirty "G" Word

Lets get the G word out of the way. God. This is a very personal and emotive issue, so all I will say is this: You can believe in God, and still have an internal locus of control (I say this as an agnostic).

So there are two ways to look at it.

1. "I have to do what God/the scriptures say, or I will be punished. Nothing happens without Gods will."

2. "God has put me on Earth, so I can be the best person I can. It is my duty to help my fellow humans and bring joy to the world."

One is an external thinking, one is internal. I'll let you decide which is which.

If you are an atheist, that doesn't mean your locus of control is internal. Many atheists believe in conspiracy theories, and are screaming about how all those foreigners are stealing their jobs. They are as much victims of fate as those who believe that some dead scripture controls their life.

So, why does the locus of control matter again?

I would like to come back to the criticism that people face bullies in the outside world, and can't be blamed. My thinking is that we should accept responsibility for our lives. So if we are in a bad situation, it's partly our fault.

It's easier to understand why, once you know about the locus of control. People who have an internal locus of control have a very strong emotional strength, that makes them impervious to attacks.

We live in a world full of bullies, racists, sexists, and all other -ists. You can't stop being their target. But people with an internal thinking will always think, "What did I do wrong here, and how can I avoid this situation in the future?" While someone external will think, "Why me? What have I done to deserve this? The story of my life."

As an aside, when I was newly married, my wife burnt some food by mistake. She said "Why does it always happen to me?"

I went crazy, and warned her never to use words like that again. Someone might have thought I was overreacting, but I wasn't. People who says things like "Why does it happen to me," have an external locus. They believe that there is an it in the outside world that comes in the window and does things to them. A person with an internal locus would say, "Hey, I was distracted. I won't watch TV while cooking in the future." You might still burn your food, but you are not blaming an outside it, rather you are accepting that you are the master of your life, and you have the power to change your future. Watch your language- it betrays you.

For someone with internal thinking, even if they face a bad situation, they will immediately bounce back. Think of it like a marine commando. If you surprise punch a marine, he will go down. But he'll be back up in second. And even though he'll be in pain, he'll be ready to take you on. You'll never land a second punch.

As some who went from an extremely external locus to an internal one, trust me when I say this: That's the sort of strength you get by having an internal locus of control. You will still face tough conditions, but they will never keep you down. Emotionally speaking, would you rather be a fat accountant or a marine commando?

So watch your language, and watch your thinking. That's what I meant when I said you need to learn how to think. Learn to think internal: "What have I done to put myself in this situation?" Even if it isn't your fault, as it usually won't be, thinking like this will show you the way to escape. While all whining will get you is the company of other whiners.

Goodbye for now

Goodbye for now.

And **Remember to be AWESOME!**

www.ingramcontent.com/pod-product-compliance
Lightning Source LLC
Chambersburg PA
CBHW071817200526
45169CB00018B/355